THE INVESTOR
AND THE
SECURITIES ACT

A Da Capo Press Reprint Series

FRANKLIN D. ROOSEVELT
AND THE ERA OF THE NEW DEAL

GENERAL EDITOR : FRANK FREIDEL
Harvard University

THE INVESTOR
AND THE
SECURITIES ACT

By Homer Cherrington

DA CAPO PRESS · NEW YORK · 1973

Library of Congress Cataloging in Publication Data

Cherrington, Homer Virgil, 1891—
    The investor and the Securities act.

    (Franklin D. Roosevelt and the era of the New Deal)
    Original ed. issued in series: Studies in economics.
    Bibliography: p.
    1. Securities—United States. 2. Corporation law—
United States. 3. United States. Securities and
Exchange Commission. I. Title. II. Title:
Securities act. III. Series. IV. Series: Studies
in economics (Washington, D. C.)
HG4929.A2C45   1973   332.6'32'0973   78-173651
ISBN 0-306-70371-8

Published by Da Capo Press, Inc.
A Subsidiary of Plenum Publishing Corporation
227 W. 17th Street, New York, New York 10011

THE INVESTOR AND THE SECURITIES ACT

THE INVESTOR
AND THE
SECURITIES ACT

By Homer V. Cherrington

AMERICAN COUNCIL ON PUBLIC AFFAIRS

WASHINGTON, D. C.

TO MOTHER AND MARIA

FOREWORD

Although the Securities Act was unwelcome to a great many persons when it became effective in 1933, there can hardly be any doubt that the principle on which it was based has won almost universal acceptance. There is at present but little disposition to challenge the right of prospective investors to demand that any business organization which seeks their savings must provide them with such information as may be adequate for an evaluation of investment opportunities. In its basic features the law has been generally accepted by reputable issuers and financial middlemen.

No one competent to appraise the administration of the Act would expect it to continue indefinitely in its present form. As the need for basic change becomes apparent, Congress will doubtless respond with modifications. In the meantime, the Securities and Exchange Commission is in a position to make many modifications that may seem desirable. Should future appointees to the Commission entertain new points of view with respect to the policing of securities markets, modifications will undoubtedly occur, whether Congress revises the law or not. But whatever happens, it is certain that the fundamental experiences of recent years will remain a source of invaluable information. It seems appropriate under these circumstances that an examination of the law and its administration should now be made.

* * *

No private investigator can ever expect to present a wholly complete account of the work of the Securities and Exchange Commission. A great volume of material, consisting of confidential communications between the Commission and issuers, is not at present available for public inspection. Former Chairman James M. Landis has remarked that it is impossible for anyone to have a precise understanding of the policies that the Commission has pursued without knowledge of the content of this inaccessible information.

*   *   *

It is difficult for the author to single out for special mention all those who have been helpful in the assembly and analysis of the material used in the preparation of this study. He is deeply obligated to many persons associated with the Securities and Exchange Commission, the Chamber of Commerce of the United States, the financial press and the investment banking industry who have given generously of their time and advice. Moreover, he is everlastingly indebted to Miss Louise Boynton and to Mr. M. B. Schnapper, both of the staff of the American Council on Public Affairs, for invaluable aid in the final stages of the preparation of this manuscript for publication; to Miss Mary B. Humphrey for courteous and intelligent assistance in her capacity as superintendent of government documents in the library of the University of Iowa; and above all to Professor Edward H. Chamberlin, of the Department of Economics of Harvard University, for suggestions and inspiration of incalculable value.

HOMER V. CHERRINGTON

Professor of Commerce
University of Iowa

CONTENTS

Chapter I

THE SETTING FOR FEDERAL CONTROL

Throughout the decade following the first World War there were a few skeptics who, in spite of the great popularity of corporate securities, were convinced of the existence of evils in American corporation finance which held the promise of great damage to investors. It was not until after the collapse of the stock market in 1929, however, that there was any considerable acceptance of the idea that the promoters, officers, directors and principal stockholders of many corporations had been faithless in the discharge of their fiduciary responsibilities. In the light of information adduced by private and public investigation after the depression began, there were many prepared to accept the judgment of Justice Harlan Stone when in 1934 he said:

"I venture to assert that when the history of the financial era which has just drawn to a close comes to be written, most of its mistakes and its major faults will be ascribed to the failure to observe the fiduciary principle, the precept as old as holy writ, that 'a man cannot serve two masters.' More than a century ago equity gave a hospitable reception to that principle and the common law was not slow to follow in giving it recognition. No thinking man can believe that an economy built upon a business foundation can permanently endure without some loyalty to that principle. The separation of ownership from management, the development of the corporate structure so as to vest in small groups control over the resources of great numbers of small and uninformed investors, make imperative a fresh and active devotion to that principle if the modern world of business is to perform its proper function. Yet those who serve nominally as trustees, but relieved, by clever legal devices, from the obligation to protect those whose interests they purport to represent, corporate officers and directors who award to themselves huge bonuses from corporate funds without the assent or even the knowledge of their stockholders, reorganization committees created to serve interests of others than those whose securities they control, financial institutions which, in the infinite variety of their operations, consider only last, if at all, the interests of those whose funds they command, suggest how far we have ignored the necessary implications of that principle. The loss and suffering inflicted on individuals, the harm done to a social order founded upon a business base and dependent upon its integrity, are incalculable.''[1]

Significant departure from the precept that ''a man cannot serve two masters'' has been made possible both because investors have so often been ignorant, indifferent, or inarticulate and because they have been handicapped in giving effective expression to dissent when they have desired to voice it. When stock is classified for purposes of voting, when a majority of those possessing the right to vote are bound together by an informal community of interest or by a voting trust, or when a single stockholder is dominant and when other stockholders either refrain from participating in corporate meetings or carelessly grant proxies, many intelligent security holders regard dissent as impracticable. Under these circumstances, the exploiters can the more readily pursue their aims, making adjustments in their strategy as their interest shifts from common stockholders to preferred stockholders to bondholders and creditors in general.

THE EXPLOITATION OF THE COMMON STOCKHOLDERS

The principal means of exploiting common stockholders are: (a) the payment of excessive prices for the services of certain persons; (b) the payment of excessive prices for

---

[1] *48 Harvard Law Review* 8 (1934).

property; (c) the sale of stock at varying prices; (d) the sale of assets at low prices to a purchaser with whom the insiders are affiliated; (e) speculation in securities on the basis of inside information; (f) the modification of claims to assets and income.

The Payment of Excessive Prices for Services

The first person to benefit from the payment of an excessive price for services is the promoter. He is always entitled to demand fair compensation for the service he renders, but it is usually impossible to do more than make rough guesses as to the value of his contribution and he may therefore find it easy to collect excessive rewards. Officers and other employees may likewise be paid too well for their services. Although it is usually rather simple for cost accountants to estimate the value of services rendered by a machine operative, there is no formula for determining whether the principal officers are overpaid. If the profits of a corporation are increasing, it might seem that the cash salaries of officers should be increased, but there is no necessary correlation between the quality of managerial talent and profits. A corporation which is succeeding might do just as well under the leadership of less expensive officials, and one which is sustaining losses may be developing strength, under able management, for successful experience in the future.

It has often been rather simple to obscure the fact that rewards for services are large by giving favored employees something in addition to cash salaries. The most common of these devices are bonuses and options to buy stock. It has not only been possible to enshroud both of these plans of compensation in secrecy which the average stockholder

TxU

has been able to penetrate only, if at all, as a consequence of exposure unanticipated by the beneficiaries; it has likewise been possible to use these devices as expedients for giving unmerited rewards. It might seem that if a corporation has not been doing well, an executive given the right to buy a large number of its shares at a price considerably in excess of the current price[2] would be stimulated to labor earnestly for an increase in earnings with the hope that the market price of the stock might advance. If increases in price should come to pass exclusively as a result of better management, this plan of compensation would be meritorious; but an executive might be tempted to manipulate accounts in order to show better operating experiences than the corporation had actually had; and even though management might be scrupulously honest, there are many factors, besides capacity of management, which bring about changes in the market price of stock. A corporation could have a supply of materials, for example, purchased under peculiarly favorable circumstances by predecessors of present officers.

Holding companies have had extensive experience in the sale of services at high prices. The American Gas and Electric Company, for example, is alleged to have made a profit from the sale of services to subsidiaries of 71.6 cents out of every dollar charged for those services in 1927 and 74 cents out of every dollar charged in 1928. From 1917 to 1929 it made a net profit of 280 per cent of the cost of furnishing services.[3]

Many complaints have been made against charges of investment bankers for their services. J. P. Morgan and Company, for instance, paid a dollar apiece for 1,514,200

---

[2] Or the right to a bonus based on earnings.
[3] Senate Document 92, 70th Congress, 1st Session, Part 22, p. 155.

option warrants of the United Corporation. Within two months these had a minimum market value of forty dollars apiece. Kuhn, Loeb, and Company made more than five and a half million dollars from its activities as investment banker for the Pennroad Corporation. A part of this profit came from certain options which were given for nothing more than advice "against a bond or preferred stock issue and an assurance that no underwriting was necessary for a successful common-stock issue."[4] When asked to specify what service Kuhn, Loeb, and Company had rendered to justify the profit of five and a half million dollars the president of the Pennroad Corporation replied "I do not think I can."[5]

The Payment of Excessive Prices for Property

Corporations have frequently purchased property from promoters at excessive prices. It is contrary to law for a promoter to make secret profits from such a transaction, although there are circumstances under which it is not illegal for him to sell his property for more than he paid for it. To demand that a promoter forego profits would be oppressive, for increases in price may have occurred as a result of a decline in the purchasing power of the dollar, or as a result of a general increase in the demand for the class of property of which that which is sold is a part, or as a result of the fact that it possesses desirable qualities unknown at the time of the previous transfer—unknown at least to its former owner.

---

[4]Senate Report 1455, 73rd Congress, 2nd Session, p. 114.
[5]Testimony before Senate Committee on Banking and Currency. *Ibid.*, p. 114.

Whenever a promoter is free to sell property at a profit to himself, there is opportunity for exploitation of common stockholders. If he exchanges his overvalued property for common stock, he gets claim to income some of which ought, on ethical grounds, to have been made available to other stockholders; if he sells for cash, he gets money which might have been used to enhance corporate income, and hence the income of all who bought their stock under less favorable circumstances. To courts it is not profit *per se* but rather secrecy about profits that is illegal. If original purchasers have access to information as to the extent of promoters' profits, it may be assumed that they have regarded the profits as fair; otherwise they would not have become stockholders. It is only when promoters have neglected to comply with the formal requirements for disclosure of profits that they need have fear of difficulty with the law.

The Supreme Court of Massachusetts was a pioneer in defining procedure to be pursued in obtaining exemption from liability for profits. In an opinion in the now famous Bigelow case,[6] widely followed as a precedent, the Court said that a promoter may profit from the sale of property if he makes "full disclosure of all material facts to each original subscriber of shares in the corporation"; or if he makes full disclosure to the corporation through an independent board of directors; or if the stockholders of a completely established corporation, having heard the facts, give their affirmative approval at a stockholders' meeting;

---

[6]*Old Dominion Copper Mining and Smelting Company vs. Bigelow*, 203 Massachusetts 159, 178 (1909).

or if the promoter subscribes to all the stock himself.[7] It is not evident that an alert and well advised promoter would encounter any great difficulty in profiting from the sale of property in compliance with one or more of these provisions.

A corporation which is a going concern may pay excessive prices for property which it buys of its officers or principal stockholders. The principal stockholder may be a holding company which requires the corporation to purchase materials or other property at high prices or which may be anxious to manipulate the prices of the stock of some of its subsidiaries and which forces one of them to take at a high price some of the assets belonging to another.

After the stock market collapse in 1929 many investment trusts were obliged to use their liquid resources for the purpose of purchasing securities which belonged to persons dominant in their management. Some of these persons were desperately in need of cash and could not liquidate their investments in other organizations without enormous losses. It was possible for them, however, to force the investment trusts to absorb securities which otherwise would have been unmarketable and to assume responsibility for the fulfillment of certain obligations of these controlling persons, "such as participations in underwritings, trading accounts, loans, and other commitments."[8]

---

[7]Bigelow and Lewisohn had purchased some property for approximately $1,000,000 which they subsequently sold to the Old Dominion Copper Mining and Smelting Company for 130,000 shares of $25.00 stock. Some 20,000 shares were sold to outsiders. The court found that the property was worth approximately two million dollars when the corporation got it; that secret profit had been derived by the promoters; that there was a liability to surrender the profit.

[8]S. E. C., *Investment Trusts and Investment Companies*, Part III, Chapter I, p. 28 (1939). The dominant stockholders also "required these companies to relieve them of existing liabilities and obligations to their investment companies; caused these organizations to finance their clients and companies in which they were interested; and induced the making of direct loans to them, often without any collateral or upon inadequate security."

Sale of Stock at Varying Prices[9]

Corporations are not static enterprises and hence it is hardly to be expected that prices of their stock will long remain stationary. Programs of expansion or reorganization frequently require the issuance of new securities. If it is common stock that is to be sold, and if existing stockholders are to have the right to buy on the basis of the privileged subscription, it does not matter at what price the additional stock is sold so long as everybody is treated alike and so long as the sale does not violate any law. It is when the preemptive right is denied that exploitation may occur. The laws of some states permit corporations to extinguish the preemptive right by positive provisions in their charters; in other cases the right does not exist unless it is specifically provided for in the articles of incorporation. If there is no preemptive right, new issues of stock may be sold to chosen persons at prices which may be unfairly low, and which may, accordingly, deprive stockholders, not entitled to subscribe to the new issue, of a portion of their equity in the corporation. Assuming that the corporation has been successful, that it has a surplus or a hidden reserve, and that the new stock is sold for the same price as that at which the first issue was offered, portions of claims to earnings and assets would be diverted from those denied the preemptive right to the actual purchasers of the new stock.

A variation of this plan of exploitation was exemplified in the distribution in 1928 of 1,130,000 shares of stock of the

---

[9]It is not necessary that the price vary for exploitation to occur. The issuer may be much more prosperous than it was when its last stock was sold. If new stock is sold at the same price as that obtained for the earlier issue, circumstances attending its sale may result in exploitation of those stockholders denied the right to subscribe to the new issue.

Sinclair Consolidated Oil Corporation.[10] This company had been organized under the laws of the State of New York which permitted it to insert in its articles of incorporation a provision by which the preemptive right was extinguished. The stock was listed on the New York Stock Exchange, where it was selling for $28 a share at a time when the new shares were taken by the insiders for $30. This select group then proceeded with the process of distribution, making use of the trading account — an expedient which had been employed so often in the flotation of large blocks of securities. The account was opened in October and when it was closed less than six months later, the profit was more than twelve million dollars.

Opportunity for exploitation of certain stockholders through the device of the preemptive right is reinforced if the stock of the corporation is without par value. There are but few restrictions upon boards of directors in setting prices at which no par stock may be sold, except the formal requirement that prices must always be equitable. As changes in the fortunes of a corporation take place variations may be made in the prices at which successive sales of no par common stock may occur. It is nearly always difficult to determine whether any price which is chosen is equitable, and so a board of directors, permitted to deny the preemptive right, may take a chance that none of those forbidden the right to subscribe will be sufficiently conversant with the facts, or, if informed, courageous enough to challenge its judgment. It may therefore sell additional stock to a selected group of common stockholders at a price so low that they in effect get claims which, from the ethical point of view, belong to other stockholders.

---

[10]Senate Report 1455, 73rd Congress, 2nd Session, pp. 63 and 125.

The Sale of Assets at Low Prices

Although boards of directors may ordinarily sell all the assets of a corporation only with the approval of stockholders, it is customary for boards to have authority to sell substantial portions of assets without the formality of such approval. If the officers or the dominant stockholders of one corporation are heavily interested in another organization, significant assets of the one may be sold to the other at a low price. Such strategy may, quite clearly, enhance the financial status of those responsible for the transfer by increasing the value of their investment in the corporation which becomes the new owner of the assets; any improvement of this character, however, can occur only at the expense of those who have no interest in the corporation to which the assets have been sold. Precisely the same results may come to pass as a result of a merger or a consolidation the terms of which provide that stockholders in a corporation whose existence is being terminated should accept securities in another corporation in an amount not commensurate with their relative contributions to its capital.

In some instances stockholders, objecting to the sale of assets at what they regard as unnecessarily low prices, have been able to have plans for such sales set aside. This has been possible, however, only when the proposed price has been grossly inadequate. Mere inadequacy of price is not enough to justify judicial interference, however, for courts have taken the position that intervention could occur only when there was such inadequacy of price as to make the transaction border on fraud. Mergers which are illegal, fraudulent, or grossly unfair may likewise be set aside, but the farsighted and informed stockholder who is tempted to offer a challenge on any of these grounds is
TxU

likely to be dissuaded because of the expense of litigation and the certainty that the courts will deal rather coldly with his claim, laying upon him the responsibility for adducing unmistakable proof of his charge.

Many states allow shareholders who are unwilling to accept plans of recapitalization, sales of assets, mergers, or consolidations to demand the cash value of their stock. It is through formal appraisal, provided for in the law, that the value of stock is determined. In some states the stockholder may have to bear all or a portion of the cost of appraisal. Unless he happens to have a substantial investment, the right of appraisal in such states is without practical significance. In any case he must comply with the appraisal procedure in order to get any benefits, and because this procedure is unknown to the average stockholder, the benefits are rarely obtained. In some states, for example, a stockholder must be able to show that his vote was cast at the stockholders' meeting against the proposal from which he dissents; in the absence of such a showing he cannot ask for appraisal. A state may require that the stockholder file a written dissent with the corporation before the meeting is to occur. Notices of stockholders' meetings are frequently sent out only a few days before meetings are to be held, and the time available for examining a proposed change in the status of the corporation is often so short as to make it difficult for an intelligent stockholder to marshal information for judging the merits of the suggested changes. Most of the states which have appraisal laws require stockholders, unwilling to accept plans of recapitalization, sale of assets, or mergers or consolidations, to make a written demand for appraisal within a period of time specified by law. Failure to comply terminates the right to an appraisal.

Speculation in Securities on the Basis of Inside Information

There are three kinds of inside information which are useful to the speculator: information as to business secrets which management hopes it will not be required to divulge; information as to changes in the operating and financial status of the corporation about which routine reports will be published in the near future; information as to any inaccuracies that may exist in published financial statements. There is recognition by the federal government and by many social philosophers of justification for allowing corporations to safeguard genuine business secrets, but no formula has been devised for determining what items of information deserve the status of secrecy. Until some such rule of thumb is invented, opinion must be controlling and there can be assurance that those wishing to profit from speculation based on knowledge of business secrets will be no more generous in giving such knowledge currency than the law[11] or the authority of stockholders may require.

It is difficult for the insiders, even though they may have the most honorable intentions, to keep stockholders currently informed of all significant changes in the financial and operating status of their corporation. They may have knowledge of changes in the outlook for profits, likely to occur, for example, as a consequence of declines or increases in existing orders or of the prospect for modification of competitive relationships or of the likely outcome of threatened but unpublicized labor difficulty. Since there may be doubt as to the wisdom of releasing information regarding any such potentiality until it actually occurs, the issue can readily be resolved in favor of secrecy if the insiders wish to engage in speculative activity for their own advantage.

---

[11]The S.E.C. has power to decide whether any item of information required under the Securities Act shall be granted the status of secrecy.

Information as to inaccuracies in published financial statements is likewise beneficial to the speculator. Deliberate understatement of any item of value may be inspired by the wish to be conservative in accounting, but it is nonetheless just as deceptive and hence just as damaging to certain people as deliberate overstatement could be to others. A management which wishes to enable insiders to buy stock at low prices can render them valuable aid by keeping published earnings low and building up hidden reserves. If a policy of this kind is pursued over a long time, outside stockholders who know nothing of what is happening may at last sell their stock for much less than it is worth. On the other hand, costs—particularly such items as depreciation and obsolescence—may be understated and as a consequence reported income may be larger than has actually been obtained. If this continues long enough and outsiders have no knowledge of what is occurring, the insiders may be able to dispose of their stock at prices in excess of what it would otherwise bring.

Modifications of Claims to Assets and Income

When directors have authority to pay dividends by making appropriations from surplus, and there are two or more classes of stock, it may be possible to use paid-in surplus contributed by one class of stockholders to pay dividends to another. Whenever that occurs, the capital contributions of the one are used to provide the other group of shareholders with income. Claims to income may be modified, too, without consultation with those affected if, for example, the directors are required to allocate a definite portion of total dividend payments to one class of stock and another portion to a second class, and if the board is authorized to use corporate surplus for the purchase of units of any class of its own stock that it may wish to buy. By retiring a portion of the stock whose owners are to be favored in dividend distributions, the dividend available for distribution among owners of the remaining shares will be increased. The situation is peculiarly ironical if the surplus which is used in the retirement of stock was contributed by stockholders belonging to a group which does not profit by such transaction.

HAZARDS TO PREFERRED STOCKHOLDERS

Preferred stockholders have all the hazards to which common stockholders are subject and are besides confronted at times with the possible peril of being forced to surrender their claim to accumulated dividends as a consequence of an unwelcome corporate reorganization. To the preferred stockholder residual claims and unrestricted power to participate in stockholders' meetings are generally less significant than the hope of a fixed and regular income and preferential treatment if dissolution seems desirable or necessary. In exchange for such potential advantages the preferred stockholder may be required not only to surrender the voting privilege but to be ready upon appropriate notice to surrender his stock at a call price fixed in the contract prepared by the corporation prior to the original distribution.[12]

---

[12]The stockholder, then, who owns callable preferred makes the additional sacrifice of foregoing opportunity for speculative profit which might be possible if the corporation were not free to demand the surrender of preferred shares. A redeemable security frequently sells above its call price, but there are circumstances under which stock that is redeemable sells for less than it would bring if the right of redemption did not exist. This would be the case if, for example, the rate of dividend is high, if the corporation regularly pays its dividends and there is a general belief that it will continue to do so, if there is fear among investors that the corporation may redeem its preferred by calling for certain shares, and if, finally, the long time rate of interest is currently low. Under these conditions the market price of the security will be lower than it would be if, all other things being the same, the right of redemption did not exist.

Although corporations which are selling preferred stock characteristically emphasize the advantage of priority of claim to earnings, the preferred stockholder is in a weak position when the board of directors does not choose to declare dividends. Occasionally a board may be forced by a court to declare a dividend,[13] but the number of instances in which that has occurred is so negligible as to give stockholders in general very little assurance. If preferred stock is of the discretionary non-cumulative type, the Supreme Court of the United States will allow the board of directors, in the exercise of its discretion, to refuse to pay dividends even though earnings may be great enough to make such payments possible.[14] The opportunity of the non-cumulative preferred stockholder to force payment for that period is thus gone forever if the board does not choose to declare a dividend, notwithstanding the fact that the money which could have been paid to him may be reinvested under circumstances which inure to the ultimate advantage of common stockholders.

The cumulative preferred stockholder is likely to have a greater feeling of security when the directors pass dividend payments, for his contract provides that accumulated arrearages must be met before common shareholders are entitled to any dividends. The contract may, moreover, promote the preferred stockholder's feeling of safety by the assurance that certain voting rights will come into being before the corporation gets too far behind with its dividend payments. But the right of preferred stockholders to elect all or a portion of the directors under certain contingencies

---

[13]See especially *Dodge vs. Ford Motor Company*, 204 Michigan 459 (1919). The court ordered the Ford Motor Company to distribute a dividend of $19,-275,385.96 to its common stockholders.

[14]*Wabash vs. Barclay*, 280 U. S. 197 (1930).

has rarely been significant. Stockholders who have not been accustomed to voting are usually inarticulate. The inertia to which they have been subject is not easily overcome. It may be difficult, moreover, for any group seeking to mobilize opposition to the existing management to learn the names of persons having the contingent voting power and, even if they have that information, financing a campaign designed to win support for a new board of directors is ordinarily an impossible burden. Before preferred stockholders can act, the management will probably have set the proxy machinery in motion. It has the names of those entitled to vote; it is familiar with procedure in the solicitation of proxies; the financial resources of the corporation and the services of its employees are available for getting control of the preferred stockholder vote.[15]

Armed with proxies, the management may then be in position to provide for an issue of new stock with a priority superior to that enjoyed by preferred stockholders whose claims against the corporation are in arrears. Inasmuch as unanimous consent is no longer necessary for modification of corporate charters, dissenting minorities are powerless in their efforts to prevent changes which are designed to modify the priority of their claims. The new stock may be sold for cash and the proceeds used to settle dividend arrearages, or it may be offered in exchange for old stock plus dividend claims.

It is ordinarily impossible to force the exchange of preferred stock, with its dividend accumulation, for a different

---

[15]Some states have given corporations a right to deprive particular classes of stockholders of their voting power altogether. California, for example, permits amendments to charters which ''restrict, limit, create or enlarge the voting rights of certain classes of shares.'' California Civil Code, Section 362, amended 1937 c. 678 Section 2.

security,[16] but it is easy enough to devise a plan of exchange whose practical consequences may be identical with those that would have occurred had the power to force an exchange existed. On September 26, 1936, for example, the Goodyear Tire and Rubber Company published a plan of reorganization that was designed to eliminate dividend arrearages of $11.25 a share on its preferred stock. The plan provided that each share of the $7 preferred would be accepted in exchange for a share of the new $5 prior preferred and one-third of a share of common. No preferred shareholder could be forced to make the exchange but any one who did not would have to forego the cash dividend that the company promised on the new stock. Although the plan was not announced until the latter part of September, a dividend of $3 a share on the new stock, retroactive to February 1, 1936, was declared. With the certainty that the payment of dividends on the old stock could not be foreseen but that dividends on the prior preferred would be paid at once, preferred shareholders were persuaded to make the exchange and it was therefore quite simple for the company to rid itself of the old stock with the accumulated dividends.[17]

Even though a corporation may not be in arrears with

---

[16]Compulsory exchange is possible at present in New Jersey, which has a law that provides ''for funding or satisfying rights, in respect to dividends in arrears by the issuance of stock therefor or otherwise.'' New Jersey Revised Statutes, Section 14.

[17]A corporation wishing to rid itself of an outstanding issue of redeemable preferred may wish to prepare the way for redemption by modifying the call price. A recent Delaware law provides that ''any or all classes of preferred stock may, if desired, be made subject to redemption at such time or times, and at such price, not less than par, as may be expressed in the certificate of incorporation or an amendment thereof.'' The Delaware Court of Chancery, in the application of this provision, has supported a corporation which, by means of a charter amendment, reduced the redemption price of its preferred stock from $105 to $100 a share. *Morris vs. American Public Utility Company,* 122 Atlantic 696 (1923).

its preferred dividends, the power to reorganize its financial structure may be used to the possible disadvantage of preferred stockholders. Within the past ten years numerous corporations have reduced the nominal value of their common stock—in some instances preferred as well—and have thus opened the way for payment of dividends. Many dividends have been paid as a result of the establishment of surpluses arising from bookkeeping transactions incident to the downward revision of capital structures. Such plans may seem harmless but if common stockholders receive income which when properly understood is to be regarded as a liquidating dividend, the preferred stockholder's potential cushion must inevitably be thinner. When a company has the power to make such modifications, it may be tempted to be brazen in demanding acquiescence from preferred stockholders to its plan for extinguishing preferred dividend arrearages. When the International Paper and Power Company, for instance,[18] had a deficit of nearly twenty million dollars and was in arrears about thirty-six million to preferred stockholders, it proposed a plan of recapitalization whose basic purpose it was to clear the way for the payment of dividends on common stock. The company was a common law trust whose declaration of trust forbade it to pay dividends of any kind so long as a deficit existed. Although its current earnings were large enough to require it to pay an undistributed profits tax of five million dollars, if it retained its earnings, it could not pay any dividends until the deficit had been eliminated. The company might pay the tax, or it might eliminate the deficit altogether as a consequence of recapitalization. Relief from the tax could have been obtained by reducing the stated value of the

---

[18]S.E.C., Holding Company Act Release No. 641, May 5, 1937.

common stock by the amount of the deficit and by using the current income to apply on preferred dividend accumulations. Such a plan did not seem attractive to common stockholders, however, for even though the deficit might have been wiped out, it would then have become necessary for them to wait until the accumulated claims of preferred stockholders had been paid before the common stockholders could have any dividends. Management proposed that the preferred shareholders accept one share of convertible 5 per cent preferred and one share of common in exchange for each share of outstanding preferred. They could have refused to accept the proposal, but had they done so, the company was prepared to retain its earnings and pay the undistributed profits tax of five million dollars. Management was able to intimidate preferred shareholders into accepting a plan that was primarily advantageous to the common stockholders.

THE POSITION OF BONDHOLDERS[19]

The position of bondholders has often been weakened as a consequence of the negligence and selfishness of trustees under trust indentures and of the exploitative activities of reorganization committees.

Trustees Under Trust Indentures

Corporate bonds are issued on the basis of complicated legal documents known as trust indentures. Inasmuch as important issues are often sold to investment banks for subsequent distribution, it is impossible for a corporation

---

[19]The Trust Indenture Act of 1939 has presumably corrected many of the evils considered in the ensuing discussion. That Act does not apply to any indentures issued prior to February, 1940.

to bargain directly with those who are to become ultimate owners of its bonds. It is obliged, therefore, to insert in its contract such provisions as it believes necessary in order to attract the interest of those who have funds available for investment. The necessity for being concerned about what such persons will think has been greatly attenuated, however, by two circumstances: most bond purchasers never trouble themselves about the content of trust indentures or, if they do, discover that the legal complexities and implications of these contracts are beyond the grasp of all except those who are legal specialists; and trust indentures have usually been so standardized that, though some of their provisions were unattractive, the investor was rarely able to find a contract upon which he could rely, in an emergency, to protect his investment.

The difference in the timing of a contract and the sale of bonds occurring in consequence of it, together with the apathy of bondholders as to the character of the contract, strengthened the determination of trustees to have included in these indentures, rather generally, items designed to absolve them from practically every fiduciary obligation. Although many trustees have discharged their responsibilities in a spirit of fidelity to bondholders, the legal opportunity for departure from such a spirit inspired some trustees to promote their own interests regardless of what might happen to the investors for whose protection they had supposedly been chosen.

The most important departures from the spirit of genuine trusteeship have been related to recordation of mortgages, disposition of proceeds of the sale of the issue of bonds, substitution of security, maintenance of priority to claims of bondholders, sales of additional bonds under the indenture, announcement of default, and the financial relationships of the trustee and the issuer.

Recordation—Mortgage bondholders should be entitled to the protection of having mortgages recorded. It is not often, however, that difficulty arises as a consequence of failure to record an indenture, for investment banks which are asked to handle subsequent issues can be expected to have information about the prior issue and would hardly run the risk of being charged with fraud in advertising a priority which did not actually exist. Nor is it likely that commercial banks asked to extend short term credit will be ignorant of the existence of a mortgage. Failure to record mortgages has nevertheless been a source of difficulty in some cases.[20] In a few of them the trustee has been held liable for having neglected to record the mortgage but trustees have rather generally provided in indentures that they would assume no responsibility for recordation.[21] The result was that unless issuers were willing on their own volition to take care of this matter, recordation did not occur at all.

Disposition of Proceeds—The intelligent investor is influenced in his purchase of bonds by plans of issuers for the use of the new capital which they expect to obtain. And yet "there have been instances of failure to erect buildings in which purchasers of bonds supposed they had invested, of diversion of proceeds to service other issues sponsored by the same underwriter; and of other similar

[20]*e.g. Bell vs. Title Trust and Guarantee Company*, 292 Pennsylvania 228; *Benton vs. Safe Deposit Bank*, 255 New York 260; *Green vs. Title Guarantee and Trust Company*, 227 New York, Supp. 252; *Miles vs. Vivian*, 79 Federal 848.

[21]The S.E.C. found as a result of an examination of 365 indentures that trustees in 86 per cent of the cases were without obligation with regard to recordation. *Report on the Study and Investigation of the Work, Activities, Personnel and Functions of Protective and Reorganization Committees*, Part VI, p. 24.

abuses.''[22] Numerous trustees have caused provisions to
be inserted in indentures which have excused them from
all responsibility to see that the proceeds from sales of
bonds are applied in accordance with pledges in a trust
indenture.[23] Even though there are no such provisions,
trustees have been free from liability unless bound by the
assumption of responsibility. Courts have taken the position that unless a trustee has overtly or by implication assumed an obligation to accept the cash obtained from the
sale of a bond issue and to supervise its investment, it is
free from any duty to observe the use to which the corporation puts its fresh supply of capital.[24]

Substitution of Security—It is customary for mortgage
and collateral trust bonds to be issued on the basis of contracts permitting the withdrawal of property which is
pledged as security, provided other property is pledged to
take its place. The circumstances under which substitution may occur are ordinarily made a part of the indenture
in every such case. To forbid substitution might result in
unfairness both to the corporation and to the bondholders.
Certain property may be declining in value and failure
to sell might result in disaster; or there may be property for which a high price has been offered, and the
sale of it might enable the corporation to increase
the security of bondholders. It would not be consonant
with sound financial policy to forbid the substitution of
collateral or other property, but to grant the right of substitution is to open the way for weakening the position of
bondholders unless there is a satisfactory formula for sub-

---

[22]*Ibid.*, p. 30.
[23]This was the case in 222 instances out of 413 examined by the S.E.C.
Ibid., p. 29.
[24]In only 95 cases out of 395 examined did the S.E.C. find that trustees had
assumed such a responsibility. *Ibid.*, p. 30.

stitution and adequate supervision over its application. In 1929 Kreuger & Toll sold debentures[25] on the basis of a trust indenture which allowed withdrawal of pledged securities provided deposits of other securities were made in accordance with a formula which required that the aggregate par value of the entire collateral should be twenty per cent greater than the par value of outstanding debentures; that the income from the entire collateral should be twenty per cent greater at the time of any deposit than the interest charges on the debentures; and that securities selected for substitution should be chosen from certain specified categories. Among the securities eligible for use in substitutions were bonds that had been issued or guaranteed by any government having jurisdiction over as many as 300,000 people. There was no requirement that the government whose bonds were substituted should have good credit nor that the market value of securities pledged should bear any fixed ratio to the par value of the debentures nor that the income from collateral should not be permitted to fall below a fixed amount at any time subsequent to the date of deposit. Early in 1933 the collateral behind these bonds had a market value of approximately $9,750,-000 from which an annual income of $628,350 was being obtained. Had the original collateral been retained, it would have been worth $24,500,000 and would have been yielding an annual income of $1,681,500.[26]

Maintenance of Priority to Claims—It is customary for corporations which issue debentures to promise that no additional obligations will be issued which do not permit the debenture owner to be "equally and ratably" secured. If such a promise has meaning to the average investor, it sig-

---

[25]Although known as debentures they were in reality collateral trust bonds.
[26]Testimony of Dr. Max Winkler, Senate Report 1455 *op. cit.*, p. 122 ff.

nifies the intention of the issuer to create no debt which will give the new creditors a claim prior to that accorded to the debenture holders. A corporation with such debentures outstanding may find that its dealings with commercial banks which have extended short term credit have become so difficult that notes cannot be renewed without a grant of security which will give the banks a claim ahead of that promised the debenture owners. The method that has sometimes been used to provide such priority of claim is exemplified in the experience of the Paramount-Publix Corporation which had issued debentures with the promise that it would not "create, or permit the creation of, any mortgage or other lien upon any property or assets directly owned by the corporation without equally and ratably securing the Bonds thereunder." But when the company found in 1932 that it could not pay certain short term notes and that at least one of the banks with which it did business was unwilling to grant a renewal, it decided to organize a subsidiary to which it transferred a portion of its assets. The subsidiary paid for this property with an issue of notes which Paramount-Publix[27] turned over to the banks as security for its short term debts.[28]

Sales of Additional Bonds Under the Indenture—Mortgage contracts may be either closed end or open end. If the

---

[27]S.E.C., *Report on Protective and Reorganization Committees*, Part VI, pp. 11-12.

[28]In 1929 and 1930 Insull Utility Investments, Inc., sold $66,000,000 of so-called debentures, pledging itself not to issue mortgages or other pledges without securing the debenture owners "equally and ratably with all other obligations issued or to be issued thereunder," but reserving authority to "mortgage or pledge any of its property for the purpose of securing loans to the company contracted in the usual course of business for periods not exceeding one year." In 1931 it borrowed $17,000,000 of various New York banks, pledging stock which it owned, thereby giving the banks priority of claim against the company. After the appointment of a receiver the debenture bondholders attempted to obtain the return of the pledged stock but their petition was denied on the ground that the notes to the banks were for periods of less than one year. *Ibid.*, p. 13.

issue is closed end, there is a maximum amount of the issue all units of which are presumably sold at about the same time. Open end contracts permit sales to occur without any specified ultimate maximum amount. There are practical limitations, however, upon the amounts that may be issued. More fundamental than anything else is the ability of those who manage a corporation to find purchasers as an issue is increased; it is, moreover, rather common practice to limit additional issues to a specified percentage of the value or price of newly acquired property. Valuations depend upon the capacities and predilections of estimators, and costs may easily be inflated if the organization which does the buying happens to be a subsidiary of a holding company and if its purchase is made of an affiliated company.[29]

The contract may make the issuance of additional bonds rest on a showing by the corporation that its earnings are great enough to support a further issue with an adequate margin of safety; but a corporation which is devoid of in-

---

[29]Illustrative is the case of the Minnesota Power and Light Company which issued first and refunding mortgage bonds under a contract allowing the sale of additional bonds in the future provided the face value of the bonds did not exceed seventy-five per cent of the cost or fair value of the property acquired subsequent to the original issue. If there happened to be any discrepancy between cost and fair value, the lower figure was to be used. Minnesota Power and Light was affiliated with Electric Bond and Share. From the Pike Rapids Company (another Electric Bond and Share affiliate) it purchased property at a cost of $3,794,685.47, the fair value of which was estimated at slightly more than four million dollars by an engineer appointed by the trustee. Inasmuch as cost was the lower figure, it was used as the basis for determining the amount of the new bonds which could be issued. Although there was no doubt as to the price which the Minnesota Company paid, there was included in that price the sum of $1,490,994.14 which the Pike Rapids Company had paid to other affiliates of Electric Bond and Share for certain services they had rendered. It is conceivable these services may have been worth nearly a million and a half dollars but holders of previously issued bonds of the Minnesota Company were surely entitled to conclusive assurance that such was the case. The record showed that the trustee relied on casual valuations made by its engineer who in work covering a period of eleven days arrived at a figure of somewhat more than four million dollars after having "weighed the essential factors relating to the various phases of his assignment." *Ibid.*, p. 26.

tegrity in its accounting policies may find it very easy to qualify for an increased issue if it is dealing with a trustee willing to accept without question uncertified financial statements of the corporation.[30]

Announcement of Default—If a corporation defaults in the payment of interest or the principal amount of the debt, bondholders will not remain in ignorance of the fact of default for long. There are, however, many types of default[31] which may occur without publicity.[32] Failure to make contributions to a sinking fund in conformity with the indenture may constitute default. Owners of bonds do not find it easy to become excited about such a breach of contract so long as they continue to receive interest payments. Because issuers and trustees know this to be true, bondholders are not always informed when sinking fund payments are omitted. Trustees have defended their unwill-

---

[30]The indentures of the Minnesota Power and Light also provided that prior to the issuance of additional bonds it was to furnish the trustee with an earnings statement showing earnings at least twice as great as the interest burden it would have after the proposed issue had been sold. Not over fifteen per cent of such earnings could count if obtained from sources other than operation of the company or of property which it had leased. In its report to the trustee it included among income which was to count in the computation of the total interest burden income from leased property and non-operating income almost three times as great as its indenture permitted. To this the trustee offered no objection, nor did it object to the inclusion in corporate income of ''earnings'' based on ''hypothetical revenues derived from hypothetical sales of power'' to one of its subsidiaries. *Ibid.*, p. 27.

[31]What constitutes default depends upon its definition in each separate indenture.

[32]The Baldwin Locomotive Company in 1910 issued first mortgage bonds on the basis of a promise that the unencumbered quick assets of the corporation would always be equal to or greater than its total indebtedness. These were obligations of the company alone, and the assets referred to were to be assets of the company. By no possible interpretation could assets of affiliates be included; and yet the trustee was quite willing to have Baldwin maintain its position on the basis of consolidated statements. Had it been forced to segregate its own unencumbered quick assets from those of its subsidiaries it would have been obliged to admit that the terms of its indenture had been violated and hence that default had occurred. But the trustee, willing to accept consolidated statements in plain violation of the indenture, kept itself in a position of official ignorance of the existence of default. *Ibid.*, p. 33.

ingness to keep bondholders informed about these and other varieties of default with the argument that default may be temporary and that to publicize its existence might lead to embarrassment or even receivership and reorganization; that the corporation, if allowed time, may find its own financial salvation; that its reputation may accordingly be conserved and the interests of all security owners enhanced. To this reasoning there is considerable merit, but a careless or negligent trustee may make use of it to fortify itself against criticism for failure to take action in a case involving deep-rooted financial difficulty. Perpetuation of an unadvertised default may mean diversion of assets which should be used to satisfy the claims of bondholders.

The Financial Relationships of the Trustees and the Issuer—Sometimes a trustee acts as a fiscal agent for an issuer. In the discharge of its responsibilities it may receive from the corporation money which is to be used, perhaps several weeks hence, for the payment of interest to bondholders. The contract may possibly provide that such funds can be employed by the agent for its own advantage during the period prior to the time when interest payments will need to be made. In 1928 S. W. Straus and Company, of New York, loaned in the call loan market approximately fifteen million dollars, only four hundred thousand of which belonged to the company itself. The rest consisted of funds which it held as a trustee.[33]

[33] Affiliated with this same house was a national bank whose common stock the trustee believed to be an appropriate investment in which deposits for the benefit of bondholders might be employed. The same house had working control of a trustee which had received a sinking fund deposit from an issuer. In May, 1931, the trustee invested the sinking fund in a bond of the issue which it had been chosen to protect. It paid a price of 95, but the bond it bought had been purchased eighteen days earlier by the affiliated house of issue for 59. The bond was dealt in on an over-the-counter basis and during the months of April, May, and June, 1931, the highest asked price was 76. That the position of bondholders was impaired by this breach of trust needs no emphasis. *Ibid.*, Part III, p. 14.

Trustees (which are frequently commercial banks) have often loaned money to issuers whose bondholders they were pledged to protect. If the corporation is in a strong financial condition, the trustee probably feels that bondholders have nothing to lose when as a short term creditor it occupies a position in conflict with its trusteeship. If, on the other hand, the corporation is seriously in need of financial help, a rescue loan by the trustee may save the issuer from receivership and if so, the bondholders may be better protected than they could possibly be if receivership should actually come to pass. Such argument would have merit if the position of the bank as a trustee never came to be compromised because of its interest as a short-term creditor. It is difficult for a bank which is in such a dual relationship with a corporation to be unselfish about its immediate interests. If the issuer is having difficulty with its bank loans, but has not defaulted on the bonds for whose owners the bank acts as trustee, it may not be difficult for those managing the bank to feel that arrangements should be made to protect its claims against the corporation even though the position of the bondholders may, as a consequence, be weakened. The Guaranty Trust Company once extended short-term credit to the Cuban Cane Products Company for whose debenture bondholders it was acting as trustee. In 1931 it became disturbed about the security of its loan to this company. The result was that the Eastern Cuba, a wholly owned subsidiary of the Cuban Cane Products Company, mortgaged practically all of its free assets, transferred the mortgage bonds to the parent which in turn used them as security for its bank loans. Through this expedient the trustee, as commercial banker, came to occupy a position ahead of those persons whose interests it had been appointed to protect.[34]

The issue is further complicated if the bank is not only trustee and short-term creditor but the owner of issues junior to the indenture bonds. Such was the position of the Guaranty Trust Company in its relationships with R. Hoe and Company. It acted as a trustee for the bondholders; as a commercial bank it was a short term creditor; and it owned a controlling interest in the company. Default on the bonds did not occur until April 1, 1932, but two months earlier than that the bank knew that default was imminent. Instead of taking steps to protect bondholders, it completed plans during the interval for the organization of protective committees which might place it in a favorable position in the reorganization that was to ensue.[35]

REORGANIZATION COMMITTEES

Prior to recent revisions of the Bankruptcy Act, beginning with the addition of Section 77 in 1933, it had been customary for courts of equity to assume much more extensive jurisdiction than at present over corporations being reorganized on an involuntary basis. Without legislative authority, equity jurisdiction in such cases has rested upon judicial precedents going back into the experience of English Courts of Chancery long before the American Revolution. The objectives of courts of equity in receivership proceedings has been to conserve the property of financially distressed organizations; to assist in tiding them over periods during which financial readjustments might be necessary; to prevent, during the period of readjustment, any security holder or creditor, as an individual or as a member of a special group, from obtaining unfair ad-

---

[34]*Ibid.*, Part VI, p. 91.
[35]*Ibid.*, Part VI, p. 39.

vantages; and, finally, upon the completion of reorganization, to transfer control of those enterprises to private management with the hope that they might continue to be socially useful. But these worthy objectives have not always been realized. In the first place the insidious practice of having friendly receivers, which has had wide use in the United States, has had mischievous consequences. Judges as human beings vary in temperament, in amenability to suggestion, in social philosophy, and in attitude toward particular organizations. Whenever there has been a choice of courts to which a corporation might turn in its search for a friendly receivership, the choice has fallen upon that court, which in the judgment of the management, would be most favorably disposed toward its nominee for the office of receiver. Not only was the receiver likely to be chosen from the management or interests closely identified with it, but it was expected that those who had been in control would be shielded, if there might be need for it, from the peril of having any evidence of mismanagement or exploitative conduct disclosed.

Immediately upon the appointment of a receiver, or perhaps even earlier, it has been customary for protective committees to arise. So far as the court is concerned these are wholly unofficial. Being voluntary, their membership is not subject to judicial control. They are organized ordinarily, at the instigation of banks which have distributed issues that are to be protected, by trustees, by persons influential in the affairs of the issuer, or by large investors. A committee must win the support of the owners of a considerable portion of the issue to be protected if it is to be successful. This it undertakes to accomplish by formulating a deposit agreement, choosing a depository, and inviting all persons known to possess units of the security to surrender them in exchange for certificates of deposit. If there is a protective committee for each of the several classes of securities, a single reorganization committee will probably be selected to formulate a plan of reorganization. After the plan has been announced, the holders of certificates of deposit will be given a brief time to register their dissent by surrendering their certificates in exchange for the underlying securities. If, however, there is unanimous approval of the plan, it will be declared effective; if the dissenters are few, the reorganization committee may buy them off for cash; if they are numerous, it may be necessary to have a judicial sale. Inasmuch as courts allow securities controlled by reorganization committees to apply on the purchase of corporate property offered at a judicial sale, the reorganization committee has an advantage, if it controls a substantial amount of the securities, and if the property which is being sold is very valuable, for there will not often be more than one bidder at the sale. In order to give the sale a semblance of fairness, it has long been the custom for the court of equity to fix an upset price, which is the minimum price at which the property may be sold.

Techniques of Protective Committees

The upset price may seem to fit the needs of justice, but it does not always do so, for the techniques which have been employed by protective and reorganization committees have frequently enabled them to promote the interests of selected groups at the expense of those security holders whom they allegedly represented. These techniques have been: monopoly of bondholders' lists; and ironclad deposit agreements.

Inasmuch as the ownership of bonds which are not registered may change without formality, it is never possible for anyone to have a thoroughly reliable list of owners of any issue which is widely held. The bank through whose facilities original distribution occurred has probably kept the names of the first purchasers; the fiscal agents may keep the names of persons for whom coupons are cashed; the issuer itself may attempt to maintain a list; but even with the best attention possible, currently reliable lists cannot be had. It is rarely important that the names be available except in very unusual situations. The issuer will need to communicate with the bondholders if it wishes to modify the terms of the indenture; committees will want the list of names when they solicit the deposit of bonds subsequent to the establishment of a receivership. Unless a committee can obtain a list which is at least reasonably accurate, it is handicapped in winning support. It will have to rely, in such a case, upon advertisements in newspapers and financial journals to get the attention of those bondholders whose names are unknown, and the disadvantages which accompany such procedure may seem so overwhelming as to dissuade those who would like to organize a committee from doing so.

It has been an almost universal practice for those having bondholders' lists to maintain their monopoly of ownership. Support for unwillingness to share these lists has rested upon the twofold argument that easy access to the names of bondholders might lead to the organization of many rival groups who through the diversity of their appeals would confuse the minds of bondholders and that, if lists were available, security salesmen or speculators would use them for the purpose of inducing owners to surrender their bonds in exchange for obligations of other organizations. Whatever the merit of this reasoning, monopoly of bondholders' lists has been a powerful weapon for control over the personnel and activities of protective and reorganization committees.

Trustees have ordinarily been under no obligation to move for the protection of bondholders, even in the event of default, without both a guarantee of indemnification and a command from the owners of some designated percentage of the bonds.[36] Commands are often impossible without access to bondholders' names. Creditors of defaulted corporations may possibly be allowed to appeal to courts of equity for protection but in some cases bondholders or noteholders are helpless. The Moline Plow Company once issued some notes on the basis of an indenture which provided that noteholders could not sue to protect their interests until the trustee, having been petitioned by the owners of twenty-five per cent of the notes, had refused to sue. The company defaulted, the protective committee won the support of owners of ninety per cent of the notes, and a federal court refused to entertain a suit by a dissenting note owner.[37] When a trustee is forced to act, compulsion will ordinarily be exacted by a group to which the names of bondholders have been divulged and that group is likely to consist of persons under the domination of the trustee, the fiscal agent, the investment bank which floated the issue, or the corporation itself.

Ironclad deposit agreements have frequently been inspired by a desire to weaken the position of the depositors and strengthen that of the committee. Deposit agreements are usually quite lengthy and complicated legal documents which most depositors never see but to whose terms they

---

[36]The percentage varies but probably averages from twenty to thirty. *Ibid.*, Part VI, p. 43.

[37]*Allan vs. Moline Plow Company*, 14 Fed. (2) 912 (1926).

commit themselves by attaching their signatures to very brief statements which accompany their bonds as these are surrendered to a depository. The depositor has often committed himself unwittingly to an agreement which makes withdrawal a practical impossibility. Some deposit agreements have allowed withdrawal, prior to the announcement of the final plan of reorganization, only upon the condition that, in the judgment of the committee, there have been changes of a significant character in the deposit agreement or in the previously announced tentative plan of reorganization. A bondholder who accepts such a contract and subsequently discovers that there is reasonable ground for a rescission suit may find it legally impossible to initiate proceedings for the return of the money which was originally invested.[38] Actual physical possession of the underlying security as contrasted with the certificate of deposit is necessary in some courts before a rescission suit can be started.[39]

But even though a committee may permit withdrawals rather freely, the bondholder who obtains the return of his security will have to pay his share of the committee's expenses and these are often high; deposit agreements allow committees great freedom in the matter of expenditure, including control over the compensation which they obtain for their services. Committees have many varieties of expense, important among which are fees paid to depositories[40] and attorneys. Since there are characteristically no

---

[38]*Report on Protective and Reorganization Committees*, Part III, p. 87.

[39]In 1932 the owner of a certificate of deposit asked for the privilege of withdrawing bonds in the amount of $35,000 in order to initiate a suit. The request was refused, notwithstanding the offer of a pledge of a thousand dollars in cash as security for the bondholder's share of the committee's expense and a promise to return the bonds within a month. *Ibid.*, Part III, p. 88.

[40]''This depository business is always one of the most important bits of patronage which a committee has to dispense.'' *Ibid.*, Part III, p. 165.

limitations upon committees in the choice of those who are to render such services, they are in position to make choices on the basis of favoritism.

The Strategy of Committees

When management is shielded by a friendly receiver, when security holders make deposits without adequate information as to what has happened in the affairs of the issuer and as to the terms of deposit agreements, when a reorganization committee is able to dictate what the upset price shall be at a judicial sale, the setting is perfect for a committee without any sense of fiduciary obligation to perform its task for the primary benefit of certain persons and certain groups. Because of their intimate acquaintance with the affairs of the corporation which is in receivership and of their familiarity with the status of plans for reorganization, it may be possible for them as individuals to speculate in the securities of the issuer with some hope of financial profit. This is relatively unimportant, however, in comparison with the opportunity of the committee or the organization controlling it to get advantages for certain groups or persons by means of a reorganization plan designed to provide them with unmerited benefits.

Such conduct was exemplified a few years ago by appeals to bondholders to accept a depression philosophy of reorganization. They were asked to recognize the existence of widespread distress and the desirability of tempering justice with mercy. S. W. Straus and Company actually published *Proposed Principles of Reorganization* which it hoped might be widely used in reorganizations of issuers whose securities it had distributed.[41] Bondholders were

---

[41]*Ibid.*, Part III, p. 257.

asked to be merciful, to consent to a scaling down of indebtedness, to accept income bonds and common stock in some instances (but to allow the holders of junior securities to obtain a portion of the common stock), and to consent to the establishment of a voting trust, allowing the reorganization committee in each case to choose the voting trustee.

Thoroughgoing control over a reorganization is likely to mean control over the successor company. If there is a voting trust, dominated by the reorganization committee or some interest affiliated with it, control can be complete. Insurance contracts may then be given to favorites; officers and directors who are chosen may be friends or associates of the organizers, and if the trustee has controlled the committee, it is likely to be chosen to protect the interests of bondholders whenever new bonds are to be issued. The setting may be right, too, for inclusion in new indentures of provisions authorizing modifications upon the affirmative approval of the owners of some designated percentage of the bonds.[42]

---

[42]Seventy-five per cent is a frequent figure. *Ibid.*, Part III, p. 226.

CHAPTER II

PROPOSALS FOR REFORM PRIOR TO 1933

Prior to the opening of the present century the only manifestation of public interest in the social control of corporations was that which had resulted from attempts of railroads and industrial organizations to establish themselves in positions of monopoly. Of the federal laws relating to corporations in general there was none of special significance at the close of the 19th century except the Act of 1887 to Regulate Commerce and the Sherman Anti-Trust Act of 1890. At the beginning of the century fresh interest in the trust problem was aroused. Certain of the proposed solutions foreshadowed the employment of policies ultimately embodied in the Securities Act of 1933. To a consideration of these policies it is now necessary to devote some attention, if the genesis of contemporary securities legislation is to be brought into clear relief.

A third of a century ago a few thoughtful students had concluded that an important reason for the existence of industrial combinations was the secretiveness of monopolistic organizations with respect to financial policies and practices, coupled frequently with outright efforts to deceive both the public and investors. If compulsory publicity could be introduced, intelligent investors, it was believed, might better appraise the value of securities, and the public would be better guided in the formulation and application of policies designed to relieve consumers from the necessity of paying excessive prices for certain products.

PROPOSALS OF THE INDUSTRIAL COMMISSION FOR
FINANCIAL REFORM

The United States Industrial Commission proposed that
corporations should be required to publish all material facts
which might be of value to investors and to the public in
the development of social policy. This broad objective it
expected to accomplish by specifying the subjects upon
which a minimum of information should be required. Promoters of corporations, the Commission believed, should
be obliged to furnish investors with relevant information
regarding such matters as the exchange of stock for property or services and all other details of organization that
might be of material consequence to the intelligent investor.
The Commission further believed that any prospectus
which did not provide a complete disclosure of these
facts or which contained untrue statements should be regarded as fraudulent and the promoters responsible for
the deceit ought to be made legally liable for their fraudulent conduct and that there should be a complete statement of all the powers of officers and directors, together
with any limitation that might be imposed upon the rights
of any group of security holders.

The Industrial Commission felt, moreover, that corporations already in existence ought to be placed under a legal
obligation to make annual financial reports to their stockholders and that the law ought to require the verification
of these reports by competent accountants. Even minutes
of directors' meetings would no longer have been sacro-
sanct had the Commission been formulating the law, for,
with appropriate restriction, it would have allowed stockholders to demand the privilege of examining such records. The very large corporations it would have "required

to publish annually a properly audited report, showing in reasonable detail their assets and liabilities, with profit or loss; such report and audit under oath to be subject to Government inspection."[1]

OTHER PROPOSALS

The Commissioner of Corporations in 1904 was of the opinion that "secrecy and dishonesty in promotion, over-capitalization, unfair discrimination by means of transportation and other rebates, unfair and predatory competition, secrecy of corporate administration and misleading or dishonest financial statements"[2] were the principal evils of the corporate form of organization. It was his belief that the federal government should make an attempt to correct these abuses. President Theodore Roosevelt was so impressed by current criticism of the spoliative practices of corporations that, having lost confidence in the power of the individual states to deal adequately with the problem, he finally urged Congress to take whatever steps might be necessary to bring the great corporations under the jurisdiction of the federal government. Although he believed that it was not his "province to indicate the exact terms of the law which should be enacted,"[3] he did express the hope that some effective plan of control might be worked out under the constitution, but if it should seem necessary to add an amendment to the constitution in order to give the federal government adequate powers, he would certainly not be averse to taking such a step. Although Congress took no action on this subject, public interest was of such

---

[1]For comment on federal incorporation see Volume 19, Industrial Commission Report, p. 650 (1900).

[2]Annual report of the Commissioner of Corporations, (1904), p. 35.

[3]*Congressional Record*, Volume 40, Part I, p. 92.

a character as to inspire the Republican Party to promise in its platform of 1908 whatever modification of law might be required to give the "federal government greater supervision and control over, and secure greater publicity in, the management of that class of corporations engaged in interstate commerce having power and opportunity to effect monopolies." In an effort to fulfill this pledge President Taft in a message on January 7, 1910, urged Congress to enact legislation "providing for the formation of corporations to engage in trade and commerce among the States, and with foreign nations, protecting them from undue interference by the States, and regulating their activities so as to prevent the recurrence under national auspices of those abuses which have arisen under State control."[4] He also recommended a law which would deny to railroads the privilege of selling stock for a consideration of less than par; which would subject to public supervision the issuance of notes having a life of more than twelve months; and which would permit the flotation of stocks and bonds arising from reorganizations only after the Interstate Commerce Commission had given its approval. But Congress took no action on any of these suggestions.[5]

RECOMMENDATION OF PRESIDENT WILSON

President Wilson asked Congress to give the Interstate Commerce Commission power to regulate the future long-term financing of railroads doing an interstate business but because of the War action was deferred until 1920. Since then interstate railroads have been required to get the as-

---

[4]Senate Document 92, Part 69-A, 70th Congress, 1st Session, p. 18.

[5]After the Progressive Party declared for federal incorporation in 1912 President Taft changed his mind and declared that such a policy "would create the most monstrous monopoly of power in the history of the world."

sent of the Interstate Commerce Commission for the issuance of stocks and bonds or for the creation of short-term obligations with a life in excess of two years or in an amount greater than five per cent of the aggregate par value of stocks and bonds outstanding.

CAPITAL ISSUES COMMITTEE

It was our participation in the first World War that led to formal federal control over the issuance of securities. By an act of Congress[6] the Capital Issues Committee was established for the purpose of attempting to direct capital into those channels which might be most useful in winning the war. From May 17 to November 10, 1918, the Committee passed upon 2,289 applications, involving $2,564,021,000, of which issues amounting to $499,218,000 were disapproved. Cooperating with the Capital Issues Committee was a committee in each Federal Reserve District which made a "preliminary investigation and report on the personnel and financial methods of the various applicants and on questions of local necessity."[7]

Immediately after the war ended the Capital Issues Committee was discontinued, but in its report to Congress it expressed the opinion that

"federal supervision of security issues, here undertaken for the first time, should be continued by some public agency, preferably by one of the Government departments, in such a form as to check the traffic in doubtful securities, while imposing no undue restrictions upon the financing of legitimate industry.

"At no time has the obligation been so definitely placed upon the Government to protect the public from financial exploitation by reckless or unscrupulous promoters. The field has been greatly enlarged by the wide distribution of Liberty bonds, and the purveyor

[6]April 5, 1918.
[7]House Document 1485, 65th Congress, 3rd Session.

of stocks and bonds is no longer put to the necessity of seeking out a select list of prospective purchasers with money to invest. He now has the entire American public, and the transaction becomes one of persuasion to trade—to trade a Government bond bearing a low rate of interest for stocks or bonds baited with high promise of high rate of return and prospect of sudden riches."[8]

During the period from the close of the War until 1933 many bills designed to protect the investor were introduced in Congress. In general these bills sought to accomplish one or more of the following objectives: publicity of important data based upon the actual or prospective experiences of issuing corporations; the prevention of fraud; federal assistance to the individual states in the enforcement of state blue-sky laws. These three different patterns were exemplified in bills presented by Congressman Taylor, by Congressman Volstead, and by Congressman Denison.

THE TAYLOR BILL[9]

The Taylor bill was inspired by the Capital Issues Committee, by the Secretary of the Treasury, and by the Federal Trade Commission. The official concern of the Secretary of the Treasury had been stimulated by circumstances prevailing in the market for long-time government bonds. It was the belief of some financial experts that the low prices of Governments had resulted in part from the fact that many persons were being induced to exchange them for securities of doubtful value. The Treasury was interested in additional long-time financing which it faced with embarrassment because of weakness in the government bond market. If investors could only be made to see the risks they were taking in the purchase of securities which

---

[8]*Ibid.*
[9]H. R. 188, 66th Congress, 1st Session.

were being floated through high pressure strategy, the position of the Treasury might possibly be strengthened as it undertook the sale of long-time obligations.

The Federal Trade Commission was interested because it had already assumed some slight measure of responsibility for attempting to stop the sale of worthless securities.[10] Its position was difficult, however, because the Commission could not possibly keep up with the activities of an entire army of security sellers who worked with great speed and moved rapidly from one place to another; control over security flotations was only a minor part of its work; and the legal basis for intervention was questionable. Mr. Huston Thompson, a member of the Federal Trade Commission at the time of its early interest in controlling the sale of worthless securities, in testimony before a Senate committee in 1933[11] said that although the Federal Trade Commission had blocked the sales of "millions of dollars of wildcat securities and had sent many wildcatters to jail," he was doubtful of the constitutional authority of the Commission to engage in such activity.

Had the Taylor bill become law, it would have required registration with the Treasury Department of every issue of stock of any corporation engaging in interstate commerce or having the power to do so, as well as every public offering of stock through the use of the mails or by means of any of the facilities of interstate commerce. Exemptions would have been granted, however, to those who might sell at public auction or to those who might make use of stock exchanges approved by the Secretary of the Treasury. The Secretary of the Treasury would have been empowered,

---

[10]As an illustration of the interest of the Commission see Complaint 293, F. T. C., Annual Report, 1920, p. 120.

[11]Hearings on S. 875, 73rd Congress, 1st Session.

moreover, to grant licenses to brokers, bankers, and dealers authorizing them to sell to their own customers without otherwise complying with the Act.

Prospectuses and other written references to the security being offered would have had to contain a statement of the fact that further information could be obtained by consulting the registration statement on file at the Treasury Department in Washington and with the postmaster in the principal city of each state in which the security was offered for sale. Persons buying registered stock were to have the privilege of asking for rescission of sale or damages by suing any signer of the registration statement or any person who had authorized the statement to be made if it should develop that it contained information false in any material respect. The bill would have allowed the presumption that decisions to buy had been reached as a result of reliance upon the registration statement.

In support of his bill Congressman Taylor said that it was "intended to compel the stock shark faker to make a truthful statement of what he has and who he is, and all about his scheme, so that any intelligent person may know that he is a swindler and is selling clear blue sky."[12] The proposal was not, in the judgment of its author, to be regarded as an experiment in paternalism; there was no thought that the government should go the entire distance in protecting the ignorant and undiscriminating; it was merely proposed that the intelligent investor should by force of law be given some basis for critical evaluation of investment opportunities. That even the most skillful were often forced to reach decisions supported by hazy and obscure information was attested by an insurance executive who wrote:

---

[12]Hearings on H. R. 188, 66th Congress, 1st Session, p. 13.

"I have for many years had the responsibility . . . of investing large amounts . . . in corporate securities. I have been impressed with the difficulty of finding out the true situation as to commissions and bonuses in connection with the promotion of companies and the flotation of security issues and have known of many cases in which the cost of marketing securities was extravagant and the amount received net to the corporation was such that, if the facts were known, the public could not be induced to purchase the securities offered."[13]

Notwithstanding the very patent fact that investors frequently knew but little about the financial affairs of corporations whose securities they purchased, there was vigorous opposition to the Taylor bill. Of fundamental importance was the constitutional objection. Although Congress was empowered by the constitution to exercise control over organizations engaged in interstate commerce, there was doubt as to whether this control might extend to a corporation which merely had power to engage in commerce but which in reality confined its activity to the state under whose laws it happened to be organized. One of the suggestions for meeting this criticism was modification of the bill so that its essential objective might be regulation of the interstate sale of securities. Constitutional objections could evidently have been met rather easily through the process of minor revisions; there were other and weightier objections, however, which prevented the bill from becoming law.

One of these was the argument that the proposal sought to place an excessive burden on honest corporations and investment banks. The provision of the factual information required in registration statements would undoubtedly have been somewhat expensive, especially if corporations about to issue new stock had decided to employ outside account-

---

[13]*Ibid.*, p. 146.

ants and other experts to compute and verify representations which the bill would have obliged them to make. It was to the right of purchasers to sue for damages or rescission, however, that the principal objection was made. It was alleged by underwriters that such liabilities might have either of two consequences: honest investment banks, in constant fear of suits which might be entered against them, could easily conclude that they would no longer participate in the flotation of new issues, in which event it might be expected that investment banking would be conducted by none except irresponsible and perhaps dishonest organizations; or if this possibility did not occur, investment banks would surely require larger fees, which would mean that corporations would get smaller sums of money in exchange for their stock.

A further objection to the Taylor bill was that whereas it went too far in certain respects it was otherwise unsatisfactory because it did not go far enough. Investment bankers, opposed to the provision relating to the liability of sellers, believed that the government should concentrate its efforts upon an attempt to ferret out and prevent the sale of fraudulent securities. They proposed a law which would require that "all literature, advertisements, and circulars regarding the offerings of shares" should be filed in Washington; that some agency of the government should be given authority to call for additional information regarding any offering of securities whenever that might be necessary for determining whether the "offering was made in good faith, or whether it was simply a fraudulent scheme, and if it should be developed upon that investigation that it was a fraudulent scheme, the Federal Trade Commission, or some other suitable agency" might act to protect investors by ordering the sellers to cease and desist from fraudulent activity.[14] The Taylor bill never got out of committee.

THE VOLSTEAD BILL[15]

The purpose of the Volstead bill was to prevent the sale of fraudulent securities through the use of the mails or the facilities of interstate commerce. It would have given the Attorney General of the United States power to require those suspected of perpetrating fraud to file with the Department of Justice whatever information might be necessary in order to determine whether the suspicion was well founded. Had the investigation provided support for the belief that fraud or misrepresentation was being employed, the Attorney General would have been empowered to end sales through the issue of cease and desist orders, and if need be, to issue subpoenas and make appeals to circuit courts for the enforcement of such orders. The bill would have allowed the Attorney General, had it appeared that irreparable damage would occur as a consequence of complete investigation, to issue a cease and desist order at once and follow it with an investigation. Any person aggrieved by such an order would have had access to a federal district court for a *de novo* hearing. The Volstead bill never got out of committee.

THE DENISON BILL[16]

The objective of the Denison bill was to provide federal support for the enforcement of state blue-sky laws. A

---

[14]It was argued, too, that access to a registration statement would give a registrant's competitor an unfair advantage.

[15]H. R. 12603, 66th Congress, 2nd Session.

[16]See *Hearings on H. R. 7215*, 67th Congress, 1st Session. See also House Report 760 on H. R. 10598, 67th Congress, 2nd Session; House Report 132 on H. R. 4, 68th Congress, 1st Session; House Report 34 on H. R. 52, 69th Congress, 1st Session.

state might forbid the sale of securities that had not been properly qualified but a seller could avoid compliance with the state law by making use of the facilities of interstate commerce; and when this occurred the state was helpless in protecting its own citizens. Securities of sound investment value could be sold in interstate commerce without having first qualified under the laws of the state in which they were offered for sale, and the federal government would take no notice under existing law. If, however, the mails were used in the sale of fraudulent securities, victims could appeal to the federal government for whatever protection the postal fraud laws might afford. These laws were often ineffective because of the difficulty the Department of Justice had in obtaining evidence to prove that fraud had actually been perpetrated. The result was, in the judgment of Congressman Denison, that the mails were constantly employed by promoters of fraudulent schemes who were willing to take a chance that the government would never be able to catch up with them.[17]

There were, besides, other agencies of interstate commerce. Although some sellers of fraudulent securities might hesitate to undertake the merchandising of their wares within the borders of a state which had an effective and effectively administered blue-sky law, they could save themselves from difficulty with state blue-sky authorities by operating from a point of safety outside the state, and they could keep themselves free from encounters with postal authorities by employing other means of communication than the mails. The Denison bill was a proposal to close this gap by making it illegal for any person to use the mails or any of the facilities of interstate commerce for the pur-

---

[17]See testimony of Congressman Denison, Hearings on ·H. R. 10598, 67th Congress, 4th Session, p. 6.

pose of selling securities in any state until the formalities of the blue-sky law of that state had been complied with. It was to be no part of the responsibility of the federal government to suggest what the policy of any state ought to be. Each state was to be free to determine whether it wished to have a blue-sky law at all and if so, what kind it might choose to adopt. Whatever its program, the federal government would give it support.

In the minds of some opponents there was doubt as to the constitutionality of a federal statute whose sole purpose it was to promise federal aid in the enforcement of state laws. The sponsors of the bill called attention, however, to a federal statute of 1890[18] which gave to states with prohibition laws the power to make these laws effective even though as a consequence of their determination to prevent the sale of intoxicating liquors it became necessary to interfere with interstate commerce. If the federal government by positive action of Congress could delegate to the states whatever measure of control over interstate commerce might be necessary in order to make particular state laws effective, would it not be appropriate for Congress to give positive aid to the states in the enforcement of blue-sky laws? A further precedent for such support, it was argued, could be found in the approval by the Supreme Court of certain other Congressional enactments which were not uniform in their operation, notably the decision in support of that provision of the federal bankruptcy act allowing in each of the states whatever exemptions might be provided by state law.[19]

---

[18]Wilson Act of August 8, 1890, which was passed by Congress in response to the decision of the Supreme Court in the case of *Leisy vs. Hardin*, 135 U. S. 100 (1890).

[19]*Hanover National Bank vs. Moyses*, 186 U. S. 181 (1902).

The Investment Bankers' Association was opposed to the bill. It did not like those laws which required the filing of data and the qualification of securities before they might be offered for sale. It was the belief of the association that such laws were burdensome to honest enterprises and no handicap to rogues who were characteristically free from fear of all laws; that the mere gathering of information by a blue-sky commission was of little consequence to the investor because the information usually remained hidden away in the office of the commission; that it was dangerous for any government to give a blue-sky commission power to forbid the sale of securities whenever the commission believed that the proposal of the registrant was unsound; that approval of an issue by a commission was likely to be used by sellers as the equivalent of a guarantee by the government.[20]

The Investment Bankers' Association felt, however, that there were evils associated with the sale of securities which the federal government ought to eradicate. It wished the government to deal more vigorously with fraudulent securities and suggested the passage of legislation patterned after the then recently enacted Martin Law of New York. It proposed that the Attorney General of the United States should be empowered to end the activity of any person engaged in distributing fraudulent securities through the use of the mails or any facility of interstate commerce by issuing a stop order, and that the federal reserve banks should be required to cooperate with the Department of Justice in attempting to discover violation of the proposed law. As a result of modifications in the Denison Bill, relating chiefly to an extension of exemption to certain classes of

---

[20]H. R. 7215, 67th Congress, 1st Session, p. 6 ff.

securities, the Investment Bankers' Association changed its attitude from hostility to support, reserving its belief, however, that control through the federal government could best be accomplished by means of a fraud law.[21] The Denison bill passed the House of Representatives but never got out of the Senate committee. It was introduced several times subsequently but uniformly failed to attract sufficient support to get through Congress.

STATE BLUE-SKY LAWS

During the period within which these unsuccessful attempts were being made to persuade Congress of the need of federal control over the issuance of securities, most of the states were attempting to deal with the problem as best they could through the use of blue-sky laws,[22] the earliest of which was adopted by Kansas in 1911. In general, following the classification of Dr. Forest B. Ashby,[23] blue-sky acts are of two classes: fraud laws, and regulatory laws.

Fraud Laws

A state which relies exclusively upon a fraud law refuses to interfere with the flotation of any securities unless it should appear that fraud has been or is about to be committed. The State of New York[24] provides that the attor-

---

[21] The American Bankers' Association and the Mortgage Bankers' Association gave their support to the Denison bill.

[22] This popular designation of securities acts was inspired by the opinion of the Supreme Court of the United States—its first opinion on a state securities law—in which comment was made upon ''speculative schemes that have no more basis than so many feet of blue sky.'' *Hall vs. Geiger-Jones Co.*, 242 U. S. 539, 550.

[23] *The Economic Effect of Blue Sky Laws*, Philadelphia (1926).

[24] The New York fraud law is known as the Martin Act which became effective in 1921. Other states having fraud laws are New Jersey, Delaware, and Maryland.

ney general may take action to prevent the sale of securities whenever he is convinced that fraud has been or is about to be practiced. Notwithstanding the vigor and intelligence which the several attorney generals of New York have employed in the enforcement of this statute, an enormous volume of fraudulent securities has been floated in New York. Officials of the New York Stock Exchange estimated some years ago that the sale of fraudulent securities in the United States amounted to a billion dollars a year and that securities having a value equal to one-half of this sum were sold in the state of New York alone.[25]

Regulatory Laws

Most of the states have felt that, if investors are to be protected, a more positive variety of control than that employed in New York is essential; the consequence has been the passage of a great many regulatory laws. A state which has this type of legislation will allow new issues to be sold in intrastate commerce only when there has been definite compliance with its law. There are certain kinds of securities, however, the sale of which obviously does not require special social control. United States government bonds fall in this classification. There are likewise certain kinds of transactions which seem to deserve exemption: judicial sales, for example. There are other types of securities and other varieties of transactions which may properly be exempted, but, because of the gradations of risks involved and the difficulties which legislatures encounter in evaluating these risks, the problem of classifying securities and transactions on the basis of their claims to exemption has not been easy. There has accordingly been widespread di-

---

[25] *49 New York State Bar Association Reports* 234.

versity among the states in the exemptions allowed by law. The Department of Commerce in a study published in 1933[26] observed that the exemptions ''most usually occurring are found in the Michigan law.''[27]

Many of the states require formal qualification of securities which are not in the exempt classification. This involves filing with the administrative agency, frequently known as the blue-sky commission, certain detailed information which, in the judgment of the legislature, an intelligent investor would require in deciding whether to buy the security being registered. The commission is then generally authorized to make an investigation for the purpose of deciding whether the security may be admitted to sale. Until the commission gives its approval the security cannot legally be sold in intrastate commerce within the state. In numerous jurisdictions blue-sky commissions have extraordinary discretion. They may deny an application if it appears, for example that the affairs of an issuer are in unsound condition or if the issuer is not based upon sound principles or is in bad repute. Aggrieved registrants may

----

[26]This study is printed in Hearings on H. R. 4314, 73rd Congress, 1st Session, p. 90.

[27]The exemptions allowed under Michigan law are as follows: Securities: (a) Securities issued or guaranteed by the United States Government, its territories, or by any State or political sub-division thereof; (b) issues guaranteed by friendly foreign governments; (c) issues of banks or corporations supervised by the United States Government; (d) issues of public utility companies supervised by the State or Federal Government and secured railway equipment trust securities; (e) issues of educational and eleemosynary corporations; (f) issues of banks under State or Federal control and of building and loan associations organized under the laws of the State; (g) first mortgage bonds and notes secured on property within the State; (h) short-term negotiable paper; (i) capital stock of domestic trust companies.

Transactions: (a) Judicial sales; (b) sales of mortgages in liquidation of debts; (c) bona fide isolated transactions by individuals; (d) distribution of stock dividends to stockholders; (e) purchases for investment, and not for resale, by banks, investment and insurance companies; (f) subscriptions to capital stock, necessary for incorporation by the incorporators.

always appeal to courts when they believe that decisions of blue-sky commissions have been arbitrary.

Several of the states rely more or less upon the good conduct of security dealers as a remedy for the protection of investors. Every dealer must then have a license from the state before engaging in the sale of securities. Characteristically the license may be revoked at any time if it can be established that a dealer has perpetrated fraud or has been guilty of gross negligence in the performance of his duties. Many states have laws requiring both registration of securities and licensing of dealers.

Early securities laws encountered constitutional difficulties very shortly after their enactment. It was alleged that they were discriminatory; that they violated the contract clause of the constitution; that they deprived organizations of property without due process of law; and that they unlawfully delegated legislative power to the executive by establishing administrative bodies to assist with the problem of regulation. The lower federal courts without exception held early blue-sky laws to be unconstitutional.[28] These constitutional objections were overruled, however, when early in 1917 the Supreme Court of the United States gave approval to state securities legislation.[29]

Had state blue-sky laws been reasonably effective, agitation for federal control would probably have been delayed. The states were seriously handicapped, however; and, besides, most of them were never particularly enthusiastic about the enforcement of securities legislation. A major source of trouble was the limited jurisdiction of the states as a consequence of their inability to deal with flotations of

---

[28] See especially 218 Fed. 482; 230 Fed. 233; 230 Fed. 236; 228 Fed. 805; 210 Fed. 173; 216 Fed. 537, involving the laws of West Virginia, Ohio, South Dakota, Michigan, and Iowa.

[29] Hall vs. Geiger-Jones Co., 242 U. S., 539, 559, 568.

securities in interstate commerce. A state with an effective and ably administered blue-sky law might prevent intrastate sales of a certain security, but if a dealer chose to
carry on his campaign within that state from some point
of vantage outside its borders there was nothing to be done
about it unless the postal authorities might find the dealer
guilty of having used the mails to defraud. The problem
of jurisdiction was troublesome too in dealing with violators who carried on their activities quietly and moved into
other states before the suspicion of enforcement officials
was aroused.

Another reason for the ineffectiveness of state blue-sky
laws had been the willingness of purchasers to compromise
with swindlers and other violators of blue-sky laws. Usually
the most immediate problem of an investor who has lost
money on securities sold to him in violation of a blue-sky
law is the recovery of as much as possible of what he invested. If he happens to be intelligent and persistent, he
may locate the seller; and if the seller is convinced that the
purchaser is determined to have his money back, it is likely
that the seller will offer partial or complete restitution
rather than submit to prosecution at the instigation of a
blue-sky commission. "Swindlers put aside from one-tenth
to one-third of the money they get to reimburse persons
who demand an adjustment."[30] State blue sky officials are
handicapped as a consequence of this practice of composi-
tion not only because they may possibly be kept in ignorance
of illegal sales but also because of the difficulties they have
in getting persons who have participated in compositions
to testify against violators of the law.

State blue-sky laws have often been indifferently suc-

---

[30]Testimony of Morgan K. Harris of the bureau for investigation of financial frauds in New York City. See *American Mercury*, March 1932, p. 354.

cessful because of the ineffectiveness of their administration. Very few states have made a genuine effort to obtain efficient and determined administrative officers and to provide them with sufficient financial support. Commissions have often been heavily loaded with politicians without particular ability or interest in effective protection of investors. In 1931 the Chairman of the Executive Committee of the National Conference on Prevention of Fraudulent Transactions in Securities[31] said that the office of administrator "is itself often a football of politics. I am told that this year alone important changes have been made in the personnel of eighteen different offices. . . . As securities law administrators undertake their new duties and gradually attain the proficiency that makes them valuable public servants, uncertainty and lack of appreciation hover continually over their best endeavors and their finest ambitions for efficiency in an arduous and highly complicated work." At the same meeting the president of the National Association of Securities Commissioners remarked that "since 1925 commissioners throughout the United States have been changed so often that today there are, I believe, only four who were engaged in the work in 1925."

The situation might have been better had there been less diversity in the laws themselves. Greater uniformity would have been welcomed by issuers and investment bankers who were frequently harassed by the necessity of furnishing a wholly different type of information in one state from that required for qualification in another. Uniformity would likewise have been helpful to those investors who before making financial commitments found it desirable to inquire into the affairs of corporations whose securities

---

[31]Proceedings of the Fourteenth Annual Convention of National Association of Securities Commissioners (1931).

they were asked to buy, but greater uniformity would, above all, have tended to give vitality to blue-sky laws and their administration. There would presumably have been more widespread information regarding laws, for magazines and newspapers circulating in the several states could have exploited the character and advantages of such uniform legislation. Effective administration in one state could, moreover, have provided not only the example but also the stimulus for emulation elsewhere. In 1930 the National Conference of Commissioners on Uniform State Laws gave its approval to the Uniform Sales of Securities Act. Immediately thereafter the American Bar Association added its approval. But even though the states might have been persuaded to pass the Uniform Act, there would still have been a definite hiatus in social control; and the closing of that gap required new federal legislation.

Chapter III

THE SECURITIES ACT

The 1932 platform of the Democratic party promised "protection of the investing public by requiring to be filed with the government and carried in advertisements of all offerings of all foreign and domestic stocks and bonds, true information as to bonuses, commissions, principal invested and interest of the sellers." As the initial step in fulfilling this pledge the President sent a message to Congress on March 29, 1933, urging legislation that would supplement the principle of *caveat emptor* with the principle that the seller should also beware. He proposed that buyers of securities should have whatever protection might come from access to full and complete information regarding the experiences and plans of a corporation which intelligent investors require before they reach decisions to buy or to sell. It was to be hoped that this objective might be attained without imposing undue burdens upon corporations about to sell securities and without putting the government in the position of guaranteeing any issue.[1] The message was accompanied by a bill which, after rather drastic modifications, finally emerged as the Securities Act of 1933.

---

[1] A brief statement of the legislative history of the Securities Act, including a copy of the President's message, appears in the annual report of the Federal Trade Commission for 1933, p. 12.

THE SALIENT PROVISIONS

Unless specifically exempted[2] every security[3] which is to be sold[4] in interstate commerce or through the use of the mails must be registered by the issuer[5] with the Securities

[2]See section entitled ''Problems of Exemption'' in Chapter III.

[3]''The term 'security' means any note, stock, treasury stock, bond, debenture, evidence of indebtedness, certificate of interest or participation in any profit-sharing agreement, collateral-trust certificate, preorganization certificate or subscription, transferable share, investment contract, voting-trust certificate, *certificate of deposit for a security, fractional undivided interest in oil, gas, or other mineral rights,* or in general, any *interest or* instrument commonly known as a 'security,' or any certificate of interest or participation in, temporary or interim certificate for, receipt for, *guarantee of,* or warrant or right to subscribe to or purchase, any of the foregoing.'' Section 2 of the Act. The italicized portions were added in 1934.

[4]''The term 'sale,' 'sell,' 'offer to sell,' or 'offer for sale,' shall include every contract of sale or disposition of, attempt or offer to dispose of, or solicitation of an offer to buy, a security or interest in a security, for value; except that such terms shall not include preliminary negotiations or agreements between an issuer and any underwriter. Any security given or delivered with, or as a bonus on account of, any purchase of securities or any other thing, shall be conclusively presumed to constitute a part of the subject of such purchase and to have been sold for value. The issue or transfer of a right or privilege, when originally issued or transferred with a security, giving the holder of such security the right to convert such security into another security of the same issuer or of another person, or giving a right to subscribe to another security of the same issuer or of another person, which right cannot be exercised until some future date, shall not be deemed to be a sale of such other security; but the issue or transfer of such other security upon the exercise of such right of conversion or subscription shall be deemed a sale of such other security.'' *Ibid.*

[5]''The term 'issuer' means every person who issues or proposes to issue any security; except that with respect to certificates of deposit, voting-trust certificates, or collateral-trust certificates, or with respect to certificates of interest or shares in an unincorporated investment trust not having a board of directors (or persons performing similar functions) or of the fixed, restricted management, or unit type, the term 'issuer' means the person or persons performing the acts and assuming the duties of depositor or manager pursuant to the provisions of the trust or other agreement or instrument under which such securities are issued; *except that in the case of an unincorporated association which provides by its articles for limited liability of any or all of its members, or in the case of a trust, committee, or other legal entity, the trustees or members thereof shall not be individually liable as issuers of any security issued by the association, trust, committee, or other legal entity;* except that with respect to equipment-trust certificates or like securities, the term 'issuer' means the person by whom the equipment or property is or is to be used; *and except that with respect to fractional undivided interests in oil, gas, or other mineral rights, the term 'issuer' means the owner of any such right or of any interest in such right (whether whole or fractional) who creates fractional interests therein for the purpose of public offering.''* *Ibid.* The italicized portions were not in the original act, but were added in 1934.

and Exchange Commission.[6]   Registration consists of the filing of a properly signed statement of such factual information as the Commission may "require as being necessary or appropriate in the public interest or for the protection of investors."[7]   All of the items called for in Schedule A of the Act must appear in this registration statement unless the Commission finds that, "in respect of any class of issuers or securities . . . such information or document is inapplicable . . . and that disclosure fully adequate for the protection of investors is otherwise required to be included within the registration statement."[8]

Prospectuses

The following definition of prospectus appears in the Act:

"The term 'prospectus' means any prospectus, notice, circular, advertisement, letter, or communication, written or by radio, which offers any security for sale; except that (a) a communication shall not be deemed a prospectus if it is proved that prior to or at the same time with such communication a written prospectus meeting the requirements of section 10 was sent or given to the person to whom the communication was made, by the person making such communication or his principal, and (b) a notice, circular, advertisement, letter, or communication in respect of a security shall not be deemed to be a prospectus if it states from whom a written prospectus meeting the requirements of section 10 may be obtained and, in addition, does no more than identify the security, state the price thereof, and state by whom orders will be executed."[9]

Although registration statements are open to public scrutiny as soon as they have been filed and docketed, there are but few investors who are able to appear at the offices of

---

[6]The Federal Trade Commission administered the Act until July, 1934. Early in 1941 the offices of the Commission in Cleveland and San Francisco were authorized to accept registration statements during an experimental period extending to October 1, 1941.

[7]Section 7.   [8]Section 7.   [9]Section 2.

the Commission to avail themselves of their right of inspection. It is by means of the prospectus that most purchasers are apprised of the factual information about any issue which is regarded as necessary for an intelligent evaluation of its securities. If the Securities Act is to be useful in the guidance of investors, it would appear to be imperative that prospectuses should be subject to the same principles of regulation as those applying to registration statements. With a few exceptions each prospectus must "contain the same statements made in the registration statement" unless the Commission in the exercise of its discretion chooses to allow omission or to require supplementary material.[10] It is unlawful, moreover, "to make use of any means or instruments of transportation or communication in interstate commerce or of the mails to carry or transmit any prospectus" relating to any registered security unless the prospectus conforms to the standards prescribed in the statute.[11]

It is illegal to sell a security which has been registered without providing the purchaser with a copy of the prospectus, and the prospectus which is used must be kept reasonably up-to-date. Most issues are disposed of, if at all, within a few weeks of the date of their original offering. If, however, the distribution has not been completed within thirteen months of the day when the registration statement became effective, the prospectus which is used thereafter must contain information that is not over twelve months old, "so far as such information is known to the user of such prospectus or can be furnished by such user without unreasonable effort or expense."[12]

---

[10]Section 10. The Commission also has power to "classify prospectuses according to the nature and circumstances of their use."
[11]Section 5.   [12]Section 10(b)(1).

Waiting Period

No registered security may be sold until after the expiration of the statutory waiting period. The bill which accompanied the presidential message contained no such prescription. Had that bill become law, registration statements would have become effective as soon as they were filed. The modification which introduced the waiting period was based upon the twofold presumption that the Commission should have an opportunity to examine each statement critically and, if need be, to force corrections in order to give it an effective status; and that investors should have a chance to make leisurely examination of the statement in order that they might formulate more rational judgments than would otherwise be possible.[13]   Although the position of the investor may be improved when a governmental agency is empowered to examine statements critically and force modifications in them in order to promote compliance with the law, the vigorous use of such power introduces the danger that investors will come to feel an unmerited confidence in securities whose registration statements have become effective. It has, accordingly, been made unlawful for any one to represent that effectiveness of a statement is a guarantee by the Commission of the truthfulness and comprehensive-

---

[13]The Report of the House Committee on Interstate and Foreign Commerce, which studied the bill, mentioned neither of these reasons for the waiting period. Its argument was that the waiting period would be beneficial to "minor distributors, dealers, and even salesmen" who had often been compelled "as the price of participation in future issues of the underwriting house involved, to make commitments blindly. This has resulted in the demoralization of ethical standards as between these ultimate sales outlets and the securities-buying public to whom they had to look to take such commitments off their hands." House Report 85, 73rd Congress, 1st Session. In support of the argument in the main body of this discussion see the sixth annual report of the S.E.C., p. 118.

ness of the facts that have been reported or of the investment merits of the security itself.[14]

Originally the law required each issuer to wait until the expiration of the twentieth day after the filing of an acceptable registration statement before distribution could begin. In 1940 Congress gave the Commission authority "to accelerate the effective date of registration statements filed under the Securities Act of 1933."[15] In each case in which acceleration is allowed the Commission may waive the waiting period only after having given "due regard to the adequacy of the information respecting the issuer theretofore available to the public, to the facility with which the nature of the securities to be registered, their relationship to the capital structure of the issuer and the rights of holders thereof can be understood, and to the public interest and the protection of investors."[16]

The Commission has announced that, in the administration of this new law, it will be guided by "(a) The adequacy of the disclosure and compliance with the requirements of the Act, and compliance with the applicable form and instruction book and rules pertaining thereto at the time the registration statement is initially filed; (b) The advisability of permitting the acceleration of material amendments filed after the initial filing date; and (c) The character and date of information previously or concurrently filed under any

---

[14]Section 23. Rule 825 under the Securities Act provides that there shall appear on the front page of every prospectus the following statement. "THESE SECURITIES HAVE NOT BEEN APPROVED OR DISAPPROVED BY THE SECURITIES AND EXCHANGE COMMISSION. . . . (Insert name of issuer) . . . has registered the securities by filing certain information with the Commission. The Commission has not passed on the merits of any securities registered with it. IT IS A CRIMINAL OFFENSE TO REPRESENT THAT THE COMMISSION HAS APPROVED THESE SECURITIES OR HAS MADE ANY FINDINGS THAT THE STATEMENTS IN THIS PROSPECTUS OR IN THE REGISTRATION STATEMENT ARE CORRECT."

[15]S.E.C., Securities Act Release No. 2340, August 23, 1940.

[16]Section 8(a) of the Securities Act.

Act administered by the Securities and Exchange Commission or by any other Federal Agency or which is generally available to the public."[17]

Stop Orders

If the Commission finds that a statement is materially deficient, it may issue an order which will prevent the statement from having an effective status. The order may be issued before the end of the waiting period, in which case no securities may be sold until the corrections required by the Commission have been made, or it may be issued any time after the statement has become effective, thus terminating further distribution pending the preparation and filing of such amendments as may be necessary to cure the deficiencies. The stop order is an administrative injunction subject to review in the courts.[18] If any person is aggrieved by such an order, he may ask the Circuit Court of Appeals "within any circuit wherein such person resides or has his principal place of business, or in the Court of Appeals of the District of Columbia" to set the order aside.[19] The facts adduced by the Commission are to be regarded as conclusive if they are properly supported by evidence. If either party asks for permission to submit new evidence, the request must be supported by proof that the proposed evidence possesses the quality of materiality

---

[17]S.E.C., Securities Act Release No. 2340, August 23, 1940.

[18]The stop order possesses characteristics which are identical with those of cease and desist orders with which the Federal Trade Commission had had long experience before it was selected as the agency for administration of the Securities Act.

[19]The President's bill would have limited appeals to the jurisdiction of the Court of Appeals of the District of Columbia; not only would its jurisdiction have been exclusive; its judgment would have been final. Appeals to the Supreme Court would have been forbidden. The proposal was supported by the arguments that it would save the government money and that there would be uniformity in the philosophy of decisions.

and that there were valid reasons for not having presented it earlier.[20] If the request is approved, the court may remand the case to the Commission for further study.

When the Commission issues orders which are disobeyed or which are about to be disobeyed by the persons against whom they are issued, it is empowered to seek injunctions from federal district courts or the Supreme Court of the District of Columbia against actual or threatened disobedience or writs of mandamus to enforce compliance with its orders.[21] The authority of the Commission to seek injunctions extends not only to stop orders but also to violations of the prohibition against fraudulent transactions.[22]

The proposal that the Commission be authorized to issue stop orders met with great resistance, particularly from representatives of the investment banking industry. Investment bankers had long favored legislation which was suggested by the Volstead bill. Had the Volstead bill become law, the Attorney General would have been authorized to issue cease and desist orders against those suspected of fraud. That bill did not contemplate, however, that any person should have a license to engage in transactions in securities in interstate commerce or through use of the mails. The bill which was submitted to Congress in March, 1933, did provide in effect that an issue had to be licensed before it might be offered for sale, for the plan anticipated denial of the right of sale to every issue which was not qualified through the process of registration. Although the principle of revocation was retained in the Securities Act, the basis for its application was greatly circumscribed as a result of the abandonment of certain of President Roosevelt's proposals.

---

[20]Section 9.   [21]Section 20.   [22]Section 17.

Had the President's wish been respected, the Commission would at present be authorized to revoke a registration statement if the issuer had violated any of the provisions of the Act, or any authorized order of the Commission of which such person or issuer had notice; or had been engaged or was about to engage in fraudulent transactions; or was in any other way dishonest or had made any fraudulent representations in any prospectus or in any circular or other literature that had been distributed concerning such issuer or person or securities registered; or was not conducting its or their business in accordance with law; or that its or their affairs were in unsound condition or insolvent; or that the enterprise or business of the issuer, or person, or the security was not based upon sound principles, and that the revocation would be in the interest of the public welfare.[23]

It would be difficult to think of what greater authority an administrative tribunal might need in order to regulate the sales of securities in any manner it pleased. Should it wish to forbid the sale of certain securities because of its dislike of the issuer, or because of its belief that the issuer should not be allowed to contribute to further excess capacity in the industry of which it happened to be a part or for other reasons, it would almost never be difficult to find that the issuer had at some time violated some state or federal law, that it had been dishonest, that the issuer or the security it proposed to offer was not based on sound principles, or that revocation would, in the judgment of the Commission,

---

[23]H. R. 4314, 73rd Congress, 1st Session, Section 6. Except for changes *in tense*, the language here used is essentially the same as that of the bill.

be "in the interest of the public welfare."[24] Although these proposals may have seemed attractive to those who wished to regulate the flow of capital into industry, they did not seem necessary for achieving the objective of more full and honorable disclosure. The Securities Act, accordingly, permits stop orders only when registrants have filed registration statements that are materially inaccurate or incomplete.

Liabilities

There are both criminal and civil liabilities for violation of the Securities Act. Willful violations, whether they involve the perpetration of fraud, the filing of materially inaccurate or incomplete registration statements, or violation of rules or orders of the Commission, are punishable by imprisonment for no more than five years and fines of no more than five thousand dollars each or both.[25]

The civil liabilities are probably much more significant than the dangers of fine and imprisonment. Any person who owns or has owned a security issued on the basis of a registration statement containing materially false or misleading information or from which material information has been omitted may sue for rescission of sale or damages[26] provided suit is initiated within one year of the discovery of the deficiency and not later than three years after

---

[24]The implications of such authority are suggested by the testimony of Mr. Huston Thompson, a former member of the Federal Trade Commission and one of the authors of the bill submitted to Congress by the President. Before the Senate Committee on Banking and Currency he admitted that "the bill as it now stands is retroactive in the sense that it would compel all securities to be registered." Hearing on S. 875, 73rd Congress, 1st Session, p. 115.

[25]Section 24.

[26]Rescission is possible only when the security is still owned. Damages may be asked if the plaintiff has disposed of the security.

the security was originally offered for public distribution.[27]
The persons liable are "(1) every person who signed the
registration statement;[28] (2) every person who was a director of (or person performing similar functions), or partner in, the issuer at the time of the filing of the part of the
registration statement with respect to which his liability is
asserted;[29] (3) every person who, with his consent, is named
in the registration statement as being or about to become a
director, person performing similar functions, or partner;
(4) every accountant, engineer, or appraiser, or any person
whose profession gives authority to a statement made by
him, who has with his consent been named as having prepared or certified any part of the registration statement,
or as having prepared or certified any report or valuation
which is used in connection with the registration statement,
with respect to the statement in such registration statement,
report, or valuation, which purports to have been prepared
or certified by him; (5) every underwriter with respect to
such security,"[30] except that an underwriter may not be
held liable for more than "the total price at which the
securities underwritten by him and distributed to the public were offered to the public."[31] Suits may be initiated,
moreover, against any person who distributes a security

---

[27]These limitations were introduced by the amendments of 1934. The original
Act provided that suits had to be initiated within two years of the discovery of
inaccuracies or omissions and within ten years of an original offering. Had the
President's bill been passed, there would have been no limits.

[28]These are the issuer itself, "its principal executive officer or officers, its
principal financial officer, its comptroller or principal accounting officer, and
the majority of its board of directors." Section 6.

[29]A controlling person is liable unless the "controlling person had no knowledge of or reasonable ground to believe in the existence of the facts by reason
of which the liability of the controlled person is alleged to exist." Section 15.

[30]Section 11.

[31]Section 11(e). This limitation of the underwriter's liability does not exist
if he received from the issuer some benefit for his services not enjoyed by other
underwriters.

''by the use of any means or instruments of transportation or communication in interstate commerce or of the mails by means of a prospectus or oral communication, which includes an untrue statement of a material fact or omits to state a material fact. . . .''[32]

A suit for rescission of sale, if successful, will impose upon the defendant responsibility for returning to the plaintiff the price originally paid for the security. If the security has been sold, the maximum amount that may be recovered is the difference between the price at which the plaintiff sold the security and the price he paid for it, provided the price at which he bought was no greater than the price at which the security was offered when the public distribution occurred. The Securities Act has improved very materially the position of the plaintiff when he asks for judicial approval of his request for rescission of sale or damages. These improvements are the result of two different classes of provisions in the law: the plaintiff has the advantage of certain presumptions and the defendant may offer none but certain specified defenses.

Until the issuer makes generally available to its security holders an earnings report for a period of twelve months subsequent to the effective date of the registration statement,[33] the plaintiff is presumed to have relied upon the registration statement in deciding to buy the security. He may assert that he relied upon the statement even though he never heard of the Securities Act, and the defendant is denied the right of questioning his reliance. The plaintiff must prove reliance upon the registration statement if he purchased after the twelve-months earnings statement became available, but in establishing reliance he need not prove that he ever saw or read the statement.

---

[32]Section 12(2).   [33]Section 11(a).

The defenses which may be used in resisting suits for civil damages are of two different classes. First, the defendant may escape liability by an affirmative showing that the loss in value of the security can be accounted for on other grounds than the failure of the issuer to tell the exact truth in its registration statement.[34] Secondly, there are specific defenses that are available to all persons save the issuer. The issuer, like every person who is sued, may seek to prove that the alleged errors are not errors at all or if so, that they do not possess the quality of materiality and hence do not violate the Act. If, however, the statement is materially inaccurate or incomplete, the issuer is denied all defenses. It must rescind or pay damages.

Any person occupying an official position with an issuer may escape liability if he resigns before a registration statement becomes effective and if he advises the issuer and the Commission in writing that he has resigned and will assume no responsibility for the content of the registration statement. He is free from liability, too, if he can prove that a registration statement became effective without his knowledge and that as soon as he learned of what had occurred he resigned, advised the issuer and the Commission in writing of his resignation and of his unwillingness to assume responsibility for the registration statement, and that he gave reasonable public notice that he had not known of the statement's having become effective.

If the person who is sued is an expert, he may escape by proving that his opinions were not accurately presented in the registration statement or if they were, that he had made

---

[34]The original Act of 1933 did not provide for any such defense. The presumption was that any loss in value was to be attributed to the discovery of omissions from or inaccuracies in the registration statement. The right to show that the decline might have resulted from other causes was granted by the amendments of 1934. Section 11(e).

reasonable investigation and had reasonable grounds for believing that they were correct and complete when the statement became effective. If some one other than the expert is sued for false and misleading items for which the expert[35] has been responsible, the defendant may escape by showing that he had no reason to believe and did not believe that the expert had been guilty of making inaccurate or incomplete statements. If it appears that the expert had not been correctly quoted, the defendant may claim that he had no ground for believing and did not believe that the expert had been misrepresented.

If complaint is based upon some part of a statement which was not made by an expert or public official, the defendant may be absolved from liability by showing that he made reasonable investigation and that he had reasonable ground to believe and did believe that the statement was accurate and complete. In all cases the standard of reasonableness is that of a "prudent man in the management of his own property."[36] If the untrue statement is a part of a prospectus or oral communication, the person sued may show that he did not know and could not have been expected to know of the untruth.[37]

---

[35]Exactly the same kinds of defenses are permitted when a signer of a registration statement is sued for misstatements in reports of public officials.

[36]Section (e). The bill submitted by the President made provision for no defenses. The standard of reasonableness in the original Act of 1933 was that of a "person occupying a fiduciary relationship." That the purpose of this standard was to transform the relationships between issuers and their directors, experts and underwriters is attested by House Report 85, at page 5, in which it is declared that if the "imposition of such responsibilities upon these persons will be to alter corporate organization and corporate practice in this country, such a result is only what your committee expects." There was so much objection to the fiduciary standard of reasonableness, however, that Congress was persuaded to modify the standard in 1934.

[37]Section 12.

State Blue-Sky Laws

The control of the individual states over sales of securities is left unchanged by the Securities Act.[38] The President's bill would have reinforced the power of state blue-sky officials by introducing the principle of the Denison bill. The use of the facilities of interstate commerce would have been denied to all those who might wish to sell securities in any state without having complied with its blue-sky law. This proposal was rejected.

THE TRUST INDENTURE ACT

The Trust Indenture Act of 1939[39] is an outgrowth of Section 211 of the Securities Exchange Act of 1934, which required the Securities and Exchange Commission to make an "investigation of the work, activities, personnel, and functions of protective and reorganization committees in connection with the reorganization, readjustment, rehabilitation, liquidation, or consolidation of persons and properties and to report the result of its studies and investigations and its recommendations to Congress on or before January 3, 1936."[40] As a consequence of this investigation numerous bills were introduced in Congress,[41] and after extensive hearings before Committees of the House and the Senate, the Trust Indenture Act finally emerged in the summer of 1939. The law was designed to accomplish the following basic purposes: to provide bondholders with alert, finan-

---

[38]Section 18.

[39]The Trust Indenture Act is an amendment to the Securities Act.

[40]The results of the inquiry were published by the Securities and Exchange Commission in a series of documents entitled *Report on the Study and Investigation of the Work, Activities, Personnel and Functions of Protective and Reorganization Committees.*

[41]See S. 2344, H. R. 10292 and Senate Report 1619 of the 75th Congress; S. 477, H. R. 2191, S. 2065, and H. R. 5220 of the 76th Congress.

cially competent, and financially disinterested trustees; to provide bondholders with information about the meaning of significant provisions of indentures, to keep them informed about changes in the status of the issuer and of its relationships with the trustee; and to furnish a method which will make it easier for bondholders to communicate with one another.

The Act requires the *qualification* of indentures as a condition for the issuance of bonds. The first step in obtaining a qualification is for the issuer (obligor) to file certain data with the Securities and Exchange Commission. If within twenty days it becomes apparent that the information filed does not satisfy the requirements of the Act, the Commission may issue a refusal order which prevents the obligor from proceeding with its plans. As a matter of procedure, this is exactly like the practice of the Commission in preventing a registration statement from attaining an effective status. The Securities Act gives the Commission power to issue a stop order at any time after a registration statement becomes effective. The Trust Indenture Act, however, requires the Commission to restrict its interest in an indenture to the period prior to qualification. If the twenty-day period ends and the Commission has not issued a refusal order, its power to intervene has expired forever so far as any particular indenture is concerned.

An issuer which does not make use of an indenture may sell as much as $250,000 of obligations in any year without being affected by this Act. Even when an indenture is used, exception is extended to an issue of not more than a million dollars, "but this exemption shall not be applied within a period of thirty-six consecutive months to more than $1,000,000 aggregate principal amount of securities of the same issuer.''[42] Except in these two cases indentures for all bonds and notes which have to be registered under the Securities Act must meet the requirements of the legislation of 1939. There are, besides, two other classes of obligations, exempt from the Securities Act, whose indentures have to be qualified before they may be offered for sale: bonds or notes which an issuer exchanges, without underwriting expense, for other securities of its own issue which it wishes to extinguish; and securities whose issuance has been approved by a court as an incident of reorganization.

Although the Trust Indenture Act of 1939 is an amendment to the Securities Act, the philosophy upon which it is based is quite different from that of the legislation of 1933. Whereas the Securities Act requires nothing more than ''full and fair disclosure,'' the Act of 1939 establishes minimum standards for trust indentures by specifying items which an indenture must contain before it may be qualified. The proponents of trust indenture legislation desired originally to give the Commission authority to determine the standards for indentures, but so much objection was raised to this suggestion that Congress finally wrote the standards into the Act itself.

The issuer is required to provide the Securities and Exchange Commission with information which will enable it to determine whether the trustee who has been chosen is competent to act. There must, moreover, be an analysis of certain provisions of the indenture: ''(A) the definition of what shall constitute a default under such indenture, and the withholding of notice to the indenture security holders of any such default, (B) the authentication and delivery of the

---

[42] Public Number 253, 76th Congress, 1st Session, Section 304(a)(9).

indenture securities and the application of the proceeds thereof, (C) the release or the release and substitution of any property subject to the lien of the indenture, (D) the satisfaction and discharge of the indenture, (E) and the evidence required to be furnished by the obligor upon the indenture securities to the trustee as to compliance with the conditions and covenants provided for in such indenture."[43] The analysis has to be included in the prospectus which is used in marketing the obligations, and if the Commission feels that a supplementary analysis is necessary in order to provide investors with information regarding the character of any of these five items in the indenture, it is authorized to prepare its own analysis and to require its inclusion in the prospectus.[44] An obligor which is not required to register under the Securities Act must likewise furnish the Commission with information regarding the trustee as well as the analysis required of other obligors, and in addition must file such of the information and documents required of Securities Act registrants, "as the Commission may by rules and regulations prescribe as necessary or appropriate in the public interest or for the protection of investors."[45]

Trustees

Every obligor must provide a corporate trustee, authorized to "exercise corporate trust powers," with a capital and surplus of at least $150,000. If a trustee comes to occupy a conflicting position, as defined in the law, it is expected to cure the conflict or resign within a period of ninety days.

---

[43]Section 305(a)(2).
[44]The obligor may object to the supplementary analysis and demand a hearing before the Commission.
[45]Section 307(a).

The Conflicts of Interests. A trustee no longer has the freedom which it once enjoyed to serve an issuer under more than one indenture. Such service is not wholly forbidden but the circumstances under which it may occur are carefully defined. There is no conflict if a second indenture involves collateral trust bonds "under which the only collateral consists of indenture securities" or if the second indenture is for collateral trust notes supported by the securities issued under the original indenture. There is no objection to having a trustee serving under numerous indentures for a company engaged chiefly in the ownership or ownership and development or operation of real estate, provided the obligor has no important unmortgaged assets and provided further that any "indenture to be qualified and such other indenture are secured by wholly separate and distinct parcels of real estate."[46] Finally, a trustee may serve under more than one indenture if each involves unsecured bonds, provided "such other indentures or indenture are specifically described in the indenture to be qualified,"[47] but the Commission is authorized in all such cases to prevent the trustee from serving under two or more indentures for the same issuer if it believes that a material conflict of interest would be created.

Conflicts may occur, too, as a consequence of certain kinds of intercorporate relationships. A trustee may not be an underwriter for the issuer nor may it or any of its officers or directors be one of the obligors. A trustee may not control either the obligor or its underwriter nor may either of these control the trustee, nor may the trustee be controlled by the same interests which control either the obligor or the underwriter. With certain exceptions a con-

---

[46]Section 310(b)(1).   [47]*Ibid.*

flict will arise when a trustee or any of its directors or executive officers is a director, officer or employee of the obligor or its underwriter.[48]

The investments of the obligor or of its officers or directors in the trustee may be such as to establish a conflict of interest. This is the case whenever as much as ten per cent of the voting securities of the trustee are owned by the obligor or by any one of its directors or officers. No matter how small the investment of the obligor or of any one of its officers or directors may be, if together they own twenty per cent of the voting securities of the trustee, the latter is in a conflicting position. The trustee is disqualified, too, if the obligor's underwriter or any of its officers or directors or any two or more of them own as much as ten per cent of the voting securities of the trustee.

Investments of the trustee in the obligor, in the underwriter or in organizations which have a financial interest in the obligor may be of such a nature as to put the trustee in a conflicting position. This is the case whenever the trustee owns, or holds as collateral for any obligation which is in default, as much as five per cent of the obligor's voting securities or as much as ten per cent of any other class of its securities,[49] or when it owns as much as ten per cent of any class of the securities of the obligor's underwriter. A

---

[48]The exceptions are: ''(A) one individual may be a director and/or an executive officer of the trustee and a director and/or an executive officer of such obligor, but may not be at the same time an executive officer of both the trustee and of such obligor, and (B) if and so long as the number of directors of the trustee in office is more than nine, one additional individual may be a director and/or an executive officer of the trustee and a director of such obligor, and (C) such trustee may be designated by any such obligor or by any underwriter for any such obligor, to act in the capacity of transfer agent, registrar, custodian, paying agent, fiscal agent, escrow agent, or depositary, or in any other similar capacity, or, subject to the provisions of paragraph (1) of this subsection, to act as trustee, whether under an indenture or otherwise.'' Section 310(b)(4).

[49]Except those for which it acts as trustee.

conflict exists, too, whenever the trustee owns, or holds as collateral for an issue in default, as much as five per cent of the voting securities of any organization which itself owns ten per cent or more of the voting securities of the obligor or of any organization which "to the knowledge of the trustee" directly or indirectly controls the obligor or which is under the direct or indirect control of an organization that controls the obligor.

Whenever the trustee owns, or holds as collateral for an obligation in default, ten per cent or more of any class of security of an organization which to the knowledge of the trustee owns fifty per cent of the voting stock of the obligor, the trustee is in a conflicting position.[50] Promptly after May 15 of each calendar year and promptly after default by the obligor, if default persists for as much as 30 days, the trustee must make an examination of its entire portfolio of investments. It will be in a conflicting position if it holds as much as twenty-five per cent "of the voting securities or of any class of security, of any person, the beneficial ownership of a specified percentage of which would have constituted a conflicting interest"[51] in any of the cases considered in the discussion of investments of the trustee.

Position of Trustee as Creditor of Obligor. The indenture must contain a provision requiring the trustee to segregate any cash or property which it receives in settlement of any claims which it has against the obligor arising from grants of credit within four months of default. The cash or property thus segregated "shall be apportioned between the trustee and the indenture security holders in such manner that the trustee and the indenture security holders realize,

---

[50]The difference between this and the previous situation is that the former relates primarily to voting securities.

[51]Section 310(b)(9).

as a result of payments from such special account and payments of dividends on claims filed against such obligor in bankruptcy or receivership or in proceedings for reorganization pursuant to the Bankruptcy Act or applicable state law . . . the same percentage of their respective claims."[52] There are certain circumstances, however, under which the trustee may be freed from the necessity of sharing repayments with other creditors. Perhaps the most important of these is the provision which enables it "to realize, for its own account, . . . upon any property held by it as security for any such claim, if such claim was created after the beginning of such four months' period and such property was received as security therefor simultaneously with the creation thereof, and if the trustee shall sustain the burden of proving that at the time such property was so received the trustee had no reasonable cause to believe that a default . . . would occur within four months."[53]

Bondholders' Lists. At least twice a year and at other

---

[52]Section 311(a).

[53]"Nothing herein contained shall affect the right of the indenture trustee—

"(A) to retain for its own account (i) payments made on account of any such claim by any person (other than such obligor) who is liable thereon, and (ii) the proceeds of the bona fide sale of any such claim by the trustee to a third person, and (iii) distributions made in cash, securities, or other property in respect of claims filed against such obligor in bankruptcy or receivership or in proceedings for reorganization pursuant to the Bankruptcy Act or applicable State law;

"(B) to realize, for its own account, upon any property held by it as security for any such claim, if such property was so held prior to the beginning of such four months' period;

"(C) to realize, for its own account, but only to the extent of the claim hereinafter mentioned, upon any property held by it as security for any such claim, if such claim was created after the beginning of such four months' period and such property was received as security therefor simultaneously with the creation thereof, and if the trustee shall sustain the burden of proving that at the time such property was so received the trustee had no reasonable cause to believe that a default as defined in the last paragraph of this subsection would occur within four months; or

"(D) to receive payment on any claim referred to in paragraph (B) or (C), against the release of any property held as security for such claim as pro-times if the trustee requests it, the obligor must provide the trustee with all information in its possession or in the possession of its paying agents as to the names and addresses of bondholders under the indenture. Any three owners of bonds who have held their obligations for as much as six months may petition the trustee at any time they like for the privilege of communicating with their fellow bondholders. Within five days of the receipt of an application including "a copy of the form of proxy or other communication which such applicants propose to transmit"[54] the trustee must allow the applicants access to the information which it has in its possession regarding the

---

vided in paragraph (B) or (C), as the case may be, to the extent of the fair value of such property.

*   *   *   *

"(b) the indenture to be qualified may contain provisions excluding from the operation of subsection (a) of this section a creditor relationship arising from—

"(1) the ownership or acquisition of securities issued under any indenture, or any security or securities having a maturity of one year or more at the time of acquisition by the indenture trustee;

"(2) advances authorized by a receivership or bankruptcy court of competent jurisdiction, or by the indenture, for the purpose of preserving the property subject to the lien of the indenture or of discharging tax liens or other prior liens or encumbrances on the trust estate, if notice of such advance and of the circumstances surrounding the making thereof is given to the indenture security holders, at the time and in the manner provided in the indenture;

"(3) disbursements made in the ordinary course of business in the capacity of trustee under an indenture, transfer agent, registrar, custodian, paying agent, fiscal agent or depositary, or other similar capacity;

"(4) an indebtedness created as a result of services rendered or premises rented; or an indebtedness created as a result of goods or securities sold in a cash transaction as defined in the indenture;

"(5) the ownership of stock or of other securities of a corporation organized under the provisions of section 25 (a) of the Federal Reserve Act, as amended, which is directly or indirectly a creditor of an obligor upon the indenture securities; or

"(6) the acquisition, ownership, acceptance, or negotiation of any drafts, bills of exchange, acceptances, or obligations which fall within the classification of self-liquidating paper as defined in the indenture." Section 311(a)(2) and 311(b).

[54]Section 312(b).

bondholders or it must give the applicants a statement of the approximate number of bondholders and an estimate of the expense which would have to be borne in communicating with them. If the trustee chooses to deal with the application in the second of these ways, it must send to all bondholders whatever communication the applicants wish them to have "with reasonable promptness after a tender to such trustee of the material to be mailed and of payment, or provision for the payment, of the reasonable expenses of such mailing."[55] If, however, the trustee feels that mailing of the material would violate the law or would compromise the best interests of the bondholders in general, it may ask the Securities and Exchange Commission to decide whether the material should be sent.

Reports by the Trustee. At least once a year the trustee is required to send to each indenture security holder a report which shall contain information as to (1) its eligibility and qualifications as a trustee; (2) the "character and amount of any advances made by it as indenture trustee" if they have not been repaid and if they amounted to more than one-half of one per cent of the outstanding bonds under the indenture, and if the trustee is in a preferential position with respect to the collection of the advance; (3) information with regard to certain types of indebtedness "owing to it in its individual capacity" and "a brief description of any property held as collateral security"; (4) "the property and funds physically in its possession as indenture trustee"; (5) certain information as to action taken in its official capacity since the last report, including reports upon additional issues of indenture securities and release and substitution of property "subject to the lien of the indenture." These general reports must be sent to all per-

---
[55] *Ibid.*

sons known to be bondholders as well as to "such holders of indenture securities as have, within two years preceding such transmission, filed their names and addresses with the indenture trustee for that purpose."[56] A copy of each report must be "filed with each stock exchange upon which the indenture securities are listed, and also with the commission."[57]

If property is released from a lien, and its fair value is more than ten per cent of the principal amount of outstanding indenture securities, a special report must be sent within ninety days of the time any such release or release and substitution occurred. If the trustee has made advances to the obligor since the last report which bring its total advances to more than ten per cent of the principal amount of outstanding securities, it must make a special report within ninety days provided the advances remain unpaid and the trustee has a claim which may be "prior to that of the indenture securities."[58] Special reports need be sent, however, only to those bondholders whose names are registered with the obligor and those who within two years have "filed their names and addresses with the indenture trustee" for the explicit purpose of receiving reports of whatever character the trustee is required to submit. A copy of each special report must likewise be "filed with each stock exchange upon which the indenture securities are listed and also with the Commission."

Duties of the Trustee. Although the trustee may escape liability, if the indenture makes specific provision for it, "except for the performance of such duties" as are expressly provided for in the contract, and although it may rely, if it does so in good faith, upon "certificates or opin-

---

[56]Section 313(c).   [57]Section 313(d).
[58]Section 313(b).

ions conforming to the requirements of the indenture''[59] it must examine the evidence, submitted by the obligor, of compliance with indenture provisions.

If there is default in the payment of principal or interest on any indenture security or a sinking or purchase fund installment, bondholders must be advised within ninety days of its occurrence, but if there is default of any other character, notice need not be given if the indenture authorizes the withholding of notice and if "the board of directors, the executive committee, or a trust committee of directors and/or responsible officers, of the trustee in good faith determine that the withholding of such notice is in the interests of the indenture security holders." The indenture must contain a provision requiring the trustee, in the event of default, to use the same degree of care and skill as a prudent man would employ in the management of his own affairs.[60]

The indenture may contain no provisions relieving the indenture trustee from liability for "its own negligent failure to act, or its own willful misconduct"[61] but the indenture may relieve the trustee from "liability for any error of judgment" provided it was not "negligent in ascertaining the pertinent facts" and it may contain clauses which will protect it "with respect to any action taken or omitted to be taken by it in good faith in accordance with the direction of the holders of not less than a majority in principal amount" of the securities outstanding under the indenture.

The indenture may also contain provisions authorizing

---

[59]Section 315(a)(2).
[60]The original proposal was that the trustee should be required to exercise the same degree of care and skill that a prudent man would use if he were a fiduciary. The difficulty of determining how a prudent man would act if he were a fiduciary brought about a modification of the proposal.
[61]Section 315(d).

the holders of fifty per cent of the outstanding bonds to give
the trustee direction as to the "time, method, and place"
for making use of any remedy that the trustee may employ
or for "exercising any trust or power conferred upon such
trustee."[62] It may also authorize the holders of no less
than seventy-five per cent of the outstanding bonds to postpone "any interest payment for a period not exceeding
three years from its due date."[63]

Obligors

The issuer must promise to make specified reports to the
trustee and to owners of bonds. To the trustee two kinds
of reports must be made: those which the issuer is required
to make to the Commission in compliance with the Act of
1934[64] and those containing information with regard to
compliance by the "obligor with the conditions and covenants provided for in the indenture."[65] The latter are of
three kinds: evidence that the indenture has been recorded;
evidence that conditions of the indenture have been complied
with; and certificates of fair value of property released
from the lien, of securities "the deposit of which with the
trustee is to be made the basis for the authentication and
delivery of indenture securities,"[66] and of property which
is to be made the basis for an increase in the outstanding
indenture securities. Valuations must be made by engineers, appraisers, or other experts and if the property released in any year has a value equal to ten per cent of the
principal amount of the outstanding bonds, the valuation

---

[62]Section 316(a).
[63]*Ibid.* If any of the bonds are owned by the obligor or if they are owned by
any person who controls or is controlled by the obligor, directly or indirectly,
such bonds shall be disregarded in applying these provisions.
[64]Section 13 or 15(d) of the Securities Exchange Act.
[65]Section 314(a)(2).   [66]Section 314(d)(2).

must be made by an independent expert.[67] If securities[68] are "to be made the basis for the authentication and delivery of indenture securities, the withdrawal of cash constituting a part of the trust estate or the release of property or securities subject to the lien of the indenture," a certificate of fair value of such property must be obtained from an expert.[69] The engineer, appraiser or other expert is required to provide a certificate of valuation which must contain information upon such matters as the nature and scope of the examination made, an expression of opinion that the examination has been adequate for a judgment as to values, an opinion as to whether the conditions of the indenture (which the expert must have read) have been complied with.

The obligor is required to make a summary report to indenture bondholders, in compliance with rules and regulations of the Commission, upon the items which it is obliged to report to the trustee.

Penalties

Any person who willfully violates the provisions of the Act is subject to a fine of $5,000 or imprisonment for five

---

[67]Independent experts need not be employed, however, if the value of the property released is less than $25,000 or if it is less than one per cent of the principal amount of the bonds outstanding.

[68]Other than indenture securities themselves or securities supported by a prior lien against the property supporting the indenture securities.

[69]The expert must be independent if the property released in any year has a value of ten per cent or more of the aggregate principal amount of outstanding securities unless the value is less than $25,000 or less than 1 per cent of the securities. If property is to be made the basis for an increase in the issue of indenture securities, for the withdrawal of cash in the trust estate or for the release of property or securities subject to the lien of the indenture, a certificate of valuation is required, which must be furnished by an independent expert if the property is worth in excess of $25,000 or one per cent of the outstanding bonds and if the property within six months of the time it was acquired by the obligor belonged to some other person who used it in a business similar to that of the obligor.

years or both. Any person who, relying upon information reported in compliance with the Act, either buys or sells an indenture security may sue for damages if the information is false or misleading; persons sued may escape liability only by proving that they acted in good faith and had no knowledge that the statement was false, incomplete or misleading.[70]

---

[70]Section 323(a).

Chapter IV

THE BRITISH PRECEDENT

Before examining the administration of the Securities Act of 1933 and subsequent legislation, and the effect on the investor, one should understand not only the events which led up to it in this country, but also the manner in which the British have attempted to solve the same problems.

Although the English had had a long experience with joint stock companies, it was not until 1862[1] that the principle of limited liability had unqualified parliamentary sanction. The immediate effect of this new legislation was an expansion of public interest in corporate securities and more especially in securities issued by companies engaged in activity abroad. The encouragement which limited liability gave to risk-taking was so great that the opportunity

---

[1]In the 18th century there were two classes of recognized corporations in England, those operating under grants from the Crown and known as chartered companies and those operating in consequence of special acts of Parliament. The latter were the result of the era of canal development. It was expensive to organize either type of company, but the opportunities for profit from industry and trade were so great that unincorporated companies with transferable shares made an appearance. Their earliest existence was, as a matter of fact, in the 17th century. Early in the 18th century the unscrupulous promoter found it possible to make large illicit profits from the flotation of fraudulent securities. The number of such securities was so great that Parliament in 1720 passed the Bubble Act which was so crudely drawn as to leave doubt as to whether the intention was to forbid fraudulent promotions or to forbid unincorporated companies with transferable shares altogether. The Act was repealed in 1825 and these unincorporated companies were allowed to be organized under the Common Law. In 1844 Parliament passed an act requiring with certain exceptions the registration of such companies as might be formed subsequently. This legislation was repealed (1862) and there was substituted a prohibition against the formation of unregistered joint stock companies with more than twenty members or in banking more than ten unless authorized by Parliament or the Crown.

87

of the promoter who was anxious to profit at the expense of other shareholders was enhanced. In 1867 Parliament decided that companies offering shares to the public should be required to disclose the names of all persons with whom they had contracts and the dates of such contracts. The legislation was without important results, however, for it did not apply to the issuance of debentures and by a singular omission did not impose upon issuers any obligation to permit the inspection of contracts; nor was there a requirement that a company should file its prospectus with any public official; but if an investor bought securities on the basis of representations contained in a prospectus and the prospectus omitted reference to any contract, the buyer was authorized to sue for the protection of his interests on the ground that fraud had been perpetrated. It was possible under the law, however, for a joint stock company to enter into agreements through which subscribers to shares surrendered their right to sue. As a consequence of such contracts the law could be virtually nullified.

LEGISLATION OF 1900

The law of 1900 made it necessary for a company proposing a public offering of its securities to file a prospectus with the Registrar of Companies before subscriptions could be taken. There was, moreover, a legislative prescription of the content of prospectuses.[2] Agreements between a

---

[2] Each prospectus was to contain information regarding such matters as the interest of directors or promoters in property about to be acquired, the prices of all such property, the minimum subscription which directors had fixed as a condition for the allotment of shares, the commissions, preliminary expenses, and the fees which promoters were to be paid, and information as to management shares and fully paid shares. It was necessary, too, that the Memorandum of Association be filed. This superseded Section 38 of the Companies Act of 1867 which required that "the prospectus should state the date and parties to every *material* contract made by the Company, or by the directors or promoters thereof." Sir Francis Palmer, *Company Law* (15th edition), p 384.

company and purchasers of its securities to set aside any of the provisions of the act were forbidden. The law required that the prospectus contain not only the names of parties to all material contracts but information as to the times and places at which they might be inspected. For the first time it was made mandatory that all directors as well as all persons about to become directors should attach their signatures to prospectuses.

For a long time previous to 1900 many companies seeking new capital had used prospectuses in which the names of directors appeared, and for many years before 1900 courts had been willing to impose liability upon directors for untrue statements appearing in prospectuses. In 1889, however, the degree of liability had been very greatly attenuated as a consequence of an important judicial opinion[3] which held that a security owner could recover in a suit against a director only when the plaintiff was able to prove affirmatively that the director had been guilty of fraud. To establish such proof it would be necessary to show that a director had been a party to a statement which he knew to be false or about whose truth or falsity he had not been concerned. Because of the impossibility of knowing the degree of faith any director might have had in a statement at the moment he signed it, the chance of recovery could hardly ever be more than negligible.

DIRECTORS' LIABILITY ACT

In 1890 the now famous Directors' Liability Act became law. Directors and promoters were made personally liable for untrue statements in prospectuses unless they could establish one or more of the defenses permitted under the

---

[3]*Derry vs. Peek,* 14 App. Cas. 337 (1889).

Act. A director might escape liability for untrue statements if they had been based upon the testimony of public officials or experts and if he could show that he believed the representation appearing in the prospectus to be a fair statement of what the public official or expert had said. But, on a showing that the director had no reasonable ground for believing the public official or expert, liability might be imposed. Liability could be escaped, in the second place, if in case of statements not made on the testimony of public officials or experts, a director could prove that he had reasonable ground for believing and did believe up to the time of allotment of shares that the statements, subsequently proved to be untrue, were accurate. The legislation of 1890 did not, however, impose upon directors an obligation to make an affirmative examination of each item in a prospectus in order to assure themselves of its accuracy; nor did it deal discriminatingly with the quality that an untrue statement ought to possess before it could be used as the basis for a suit against directors and promoters.

A statement may be untrue and an intelligent director may know it is untrue when he signs it. If, however, the untruth cannot possibly have had any bearing upon the subsequent misfortunes of any stockholder, it would hardly be honorable or just to allow an attack upon the personal fortunes of directors merely because they were lacking in honor with respect to an inconsequential item in a prospectus. It is only material facts and contracts that are important. Perhaps no better approach to what constitutes materiality has ever been made than that which appears in the Draft bill attached to the Lord Davey Report of 1895: "Every contract or fact is material which would influence the judgment of a prudent investor in determining whether he would subscribe for the shares or debentures offered by the prospectus.''[4] In 1906 the House of Lords applied this doctrine when it held that a contract in order to be construed as material must be one "which would be likely to influence the judgment of an interested applicant.''[5]

The law of 1900 which required directors to sign prospectuses before they could be accepted for filing with the Registrar of Companies was regarded as very severe. An avenue of escape was found when companies discovered that it was legal to obtain subscriptions "on forms of application accompanied by oral statements, or by selling shares in the stock market through financiers or others, or by means of a pooling syndicate.''[6] When subscriptions were taken in these ways, prospectuses were not required and hence it was presumably possible for directors to escape liability.[7]

In 1907 the law was strengthened by making it necessary for a company with share capital[8] which did not use a prospectus at the time of its organization or which, having issued a prospectus, had never allotted its shares, to file with the Registrar a statement in lieu of a prospectus not later than three days before an allotment of any securities.

REVISIONS OF 1928 AND 1929

For almost a generation there was no further important change in the law relating to the issuance of securities. During the War the Treasury exercised a measure of con-

---

[4]Cmd. 7779 (1895) Section 14(5).
[5]*Macleay vs. Tait*, A. C. 24 (1906) 75 L. J. Ch. 90.
[6]Palmer, *Company Law, op. cit.*, p. 387.
[7]It was not the Companies Act or the Directors' Liability Act, but rather the Larceny Act of 1861, which the British applied in the Kylsant case, the most celebrated of all recent cases involving directors' liability.
[8]As contrasted with a company which is limited by guarantee; that is, one in which each subscriber guarantees a certain sum he is ready to supply in case of need.

trol over the capital market with the objective of making it easier for the government to get whatever funds it might need for the successful prosecution of the War.[9] Early in 1918 the Board of Trade appointed a special committee[10] to inquire into the desirability of introducing modifications into the Companies Act. Nothing of a significant nature came of this inquiry. The need for change seemed so urgent, however, that in 1925 the Board of Trade appointed another committee, the Greene Committee, which undertook the most thoroughgoing examination of the Companies Act and of proposals for reform that had occurred since 1895. Many changes were urged upon this committee, some of which, had they been adopted, might have been regarded as radical departures from English precedent. It was asked, for example, to suggest legislation that would require the licensing of dealers in securities. This the committee brushed aside with the observation that it had "carefully considered this proposal, and although at first sight it appears attractive, we do not find ourselves able to recommend its adoption."[11]

Although the committee was quite aware of the need for change, it nevertheless expressed faith that "the great majority of limited companies both public and private are honestly and conscientiously managed."[12] It was "further

---

[9]Control by the Treasury during the War virtually ended new issues by companies. Whenever the New Issues Committee gave its approval to proposed issues of securities, the issuers were obliged to indicate in prospectuses that no portion of the new capital was to be used anywhere except in the United Kingdom nor in substitution of money that had already been used abroad. The extent of the control exercised by this Committee is suggested by the fact that it would not sanction the issuance of new securities even when they were to be offered in exchange for outstanding securities that were to be retired as a consequence of reorganization or amalgamation, nor would it permit the funding of overdrafts or loans. 179 L. Times 329.

[10]The Wrenbury Committee.

[11]Cmd 2657 (1926), p. 49.

[12]Ibid.

satisfied that the abnormal conditions prevailing during and since the war have been largely responsible for some of the matters which have given rise to unfavorable public comment, and we are of the opinion that return to more normal conditions will tend to eliminate certain unsatisfactory features which have shown themselves in recent years."[13]

One of the post-war practices which enlightened Englishmen came to regard as especially vicious was house-to-house canvassing by dealers in securities. It came to be looked upon with disfavor partly because of the irresponsibility of certain salesmen who seemed to have no sense of obligation for telling the truth about their products and more particularly because prospective purchasers belonged to a class unschooled in the intricacies of finance and peculiarly susceptible to emotional pressure. The law was modified by a prohibition of house-to-house selling of shares.[14] Moreover, subject to certain exceptions, making "an offer in writing to any member of the public of any shares" was forbidden unless the offer was to be accompanied by certain prescribed information.[15]

Issuers of securities had discovered a very effective method of evading the requirement regarding prospectuses and hence of enabling directors and promoters to avoid liability for inaccurate statements in them. The law pro-

---

[13]*Ibid.*, p. 4.

[14]Section 356 of the Companies Act.

[15]Chief among such information is the following: (a) whether the person making the offer is agent or principal and the name of the principal; (b) date of company's incorporation; (c) capitalization and kinds of securities with statement of rights attached to each class; (d) dividends paid during each of last three financial years and if no dividends, a statement to that effect; (e) debentures outstanding with rates of interest; (f) names and addresses of directors; (g) whether shares offered are paid up and if not to what extent they are fully paid; (h) whether quoted on a recognized British stock exchange. *Ibid.*

vided that public companies should file prospectuses whenever they planned to invite the public to subscribe to their issues; it likewise provided that suits based upon untrue statements could be initiated only by originial subscribers. It was therefore permissible for a company to sell an issue to some intermediary which could then proceed with an ultimate distribution without the necessity of filing a prospectus. The intermediary alone would have the right to sue; but inasmuch as it managed to dispose of an issue within a brief period of time it would have no interest to protect and could not be expected to enter suit against the issuer. This was rectified in subsequent legislation[16] requiring the issuance of prospectuses when public offerings were made either directly or indirectly.

Certain companies desirous of being able to obtain the services of particular persons as directors and feeling that such persons might regard the Directors' Liability Act as being too oppressive had undertaken to guarantee their directors and officers against liability or to excuse them from it altogether. The Committee recognized that many directors held office because of their specialized abilities and that one who is an expert in one branch of any business should not necessarily be held accountable for every activity of the entire undertaking. It believed, nevertheless, that companies should not have the power to guarantee directors against liability for untrue statements in prospectuses. It did feel, however, that courts should be instructed to take into consideration any special circumstances, which might have attended the selection of any person as a director, in arriving at conclusions as to the extent of his liability. In 1929[17] it was made illegal for companies to guarantee their

---

[16]Section 35(3).
[17]Section 152.

directors against loss due to the establishment of liability for untrue statements. Moreover, directors who are undischarged bankrupts run the risk of imprisonment if they continue in office without sanction of the court.[18]

The popularity of no par stock in the United States had had its effect upon the minds of certain Englishmen who urged upon the Committee the desirability of modifying the law so that the use of no par stock might be permitted. This innovation the Committee was unwilling to endorse; but it did give consideration to the need of relaxing the law so that shares might be sold at less than par. And such a modification, if authorized, would be a concession to the proponents of no par shares, for one of their principal arguments is that there are circumstances under which there should be authority to issue stock at variations from the price at which it was originally sold. Although the law, as it stood in 1926, forbade the sale of shares at less than par, numerous methods had been devised and employed to nullify this provision. As in the United States, such intangible items as goodwill and patent rights had been purchased under circumstances amounting to an issue of shares at less than par. Moreover, underwriting commissions had often amounted to half the nominal value of shares. Recognizing the need for a departure from par in some instances, the Committee recommended that companies be permitted to sell at no more than ten per cent discount and that ten per cent of the par value of securities be the maximum allowed for the services of underwriters. Ensuing legislation authorized these changes.[19]

The law of 1900 had made it mandatory that the prospectus contain a statement of the minimum subscription neces-

---

[18]Section 142.
[19]Section 47.

sary before shares could be allotted. The effect of this provision was negligible, for promoters or directors could fix it at any amount they pleased which meant that it could easily be placed so low as to provide no barrier for the allotment of shares. Inability to obtain funds sufficient for the immediate objectives might result in failure on the part of the company to fulfill its obligations. It was the opinion of the Committee that the directors of each company, except those filing statements in lieu of prospectuses, ought to be obliged before seeking fresh capital, to estimate the amount of money needed for working capital and for the purchase of whatever property it might expect to buy out of the proceeds of a proposed issue; they should, besides, be required to estimate underwriting commissions and all preliminary expenses, and should not be permitted to make an allotment of shares until sufficient subscriptions had been obtained to provide for all these outlays, including the repayment of funds that had been borrowed for the purchase of property or preliminary expenses. These standards were accepted by Parliament.[20]

Probably the most important of the changes in requirements for prospectuses introduced by the new legislation was the obligation imposed on companies to furnish information regarding their recent financial experiences. The auditors of each company are required under the law as it now stands to prepare, for inclusion in the prospectus, a report of the profits earned and the dividends paid during each of the three preceding years, and if any portion of the proceeds of an issue is to be used in purchasing another business, there must be a report of the profits of that business during each of the last three years.[21]

---

[20] Fourth Schedule, Part I(5), Section 39.
[21] Fourth Schedule, Part II.

At the time of the appointment of the Greene Committee, the British, officially at any rate, did not approve of the redemption by a company of its own stock. A plan had been developed, however, to defeat the social will in this matter and it was being used currently in a considerable number of instances. Interests closely identified with a company which wished to buy its own stock in the market would organize a syndicate which purchased the stock and a few days thereafter arranged with the company for a loan of money sufficient in amount to cover the cost of the transaction. This the Committee regarded with disapproval; nor did it look with favor upon the suggestion that "in cases where creditors are not affected, the sanction of the court should not be necessary,"[22] when companies proposed to reduce their capitalization. It did feel, however, that a company should be permitted to issue redeemable preference shares under carefully guarded conditions, provided its Articles of Association allowed it; and this the law now authorizes.[23]

No longer is it possible for a small minority to interpose unreasonable obstacles to an amalgamation. The right of an overwhelming majority to consolidate their company with another is assured under the provision, recommended by the Committee and adopted by Parliament, that a purchasing company may obtain the shares of a dissenting mi-

---

[22]Cmd. 2657 (1926).

[23]Money used in redeeming preference shares may come from two sources only: profits, and the proceeds of a sale of securities offered for the specific purpose of retiring preference stock. If the stock is purchased at a premium, the excess over par must be provided out of profits. When preference stock is redeemed, the company must set up a redemption reserve which may be reduced or completely extinguished in the same manner as it would be in a reduction of capital. Only fully paid shares are eligible for redemption. A company with redeemable preference shares is required to carry in its balance sheet information as to the amount outstanding and the dates when the company will be under obligation to redeem. Section 46.

nority at the same price it is to pay those willing to sell if the latter own as much as ninety per cent of the shares, "unless on an application made by the dissenting shareholders ... the Court thinks fit to order otherwise."[24]

REGULATION IN ENGLAND COMPARED WITH THAT IN THE UNITED STATES

There are numerous differences between English and American practices regarding public control over security issuance, although basically there is great similarity. The English policy, like the American, is based upon faith in the sufficiency of adequate publicity. There are significant differences, however, between English and American practices in the application of a common doctrine that truthful publicity is an adequate safeguard for the investor. Important differences relate to:

Method of Disclosure

Whereas disclosure occurs in the United States through the process of registration with the Securities and Exchange Commission, supplemented with the compulsory distribution of prospectuses among purchasers of securities, disclosure in England consists of nothing more than the filing of a prospectus[25] with the Registrar of Companies. This official has no other responsibility than to make certain that each prospectus is in proper form, that it is correctly dated, and contains the signatures of all persons who are required to sign it. There is nothing in English experience analogous to the American waiting period, except

---

[24]Section 155.
[25]Prospectus means, "any prospectus, notice, circular, advertisement, or other invitation, offering to the public for subscription or purchase any shares or debentures of a company." Section 380 of British Companies Act.

that companies filing statements in lieu of prospectuses are required to wait for three days before making allotments of shares. The English have nothing comparable to the stop order.

Persons Affected

The British make no effort as we do in the United States to establish regulation over individuals, partnerships, controlling persons, protective committees or trusts. Inasmuch as the law applies only to public companies, private companies are not obliged to file prospectuses.[26] This exemption alone affects approximately one-third of all English companies.[27] Whenever a public company wishes to sell additional securities to its existing security owners it may do so without the formality of filing a prospectus.[28] Foreign governments are likewise free from the necessity of complying with the Companies Act.

Liability

Not only is the scope of the British law much narrower than our Securities Act so far as types of organizations and varieties of transactions are concerned; the persons having liability for untrue statements are not nearly so numerous.

---

[26] ''A private company is one which is registered under the Companies Act and which by its articles prohibits any invitation by the public to subscribe for any of its shares or debentures; which restricts the right of a member to transfer his shares; and which limits the number of its members to 50.'' U. S. Department of Commerce, Trade Promotion Series, No. 153, p. 95.

[27] Palmer, *Company Law, op. cit.,* p. 391.

[28] Section 35(5). This is contrary to American practice, except that in the United States (Securities Act, Section 3(a)), an issuer may, without the formality of registration, exchange its securities for other of its securities already outstanding, provided it pays no commission in connection with such an exchange; and it may issue its securities without a registration statement, when the new securities result from a reorganization which has had appropriate public supervision. See Section 3(a)(10) of the Act.

Only those persons who are promoters or directors or who have agreed to become directors or who have authorized the issuance of a prospectus are liable. In the United States liability must be assumed by the company, all its directors, certain officials, accountants and other experts, underwriters, and controlling persons.

In England as in the United States it is necessary to show that an untrue statement has the quality of materiality, but in England the untrue statement can be the basis of a suit only when entered by an original subscriber. In the United States either an original subsriber or any subsequent purchaser may enter suit for rescission of sale or, in case the security has been sold by the original purchaser, for damages. In England rescission does not often occur except in cases involving executory contracts. In the United States it does not matter whether a contract is executory or has already been completely executed. In England suits, of whatever character, based on untrue statements, impose upon the plaintiff the necessity of showing reliance upon a materially untrue statement in a prospectus. In the United States proof of reliance on reports in a registration statement is necessary only in case the issuer has published a financial statement covering a full twelve-month period elapsing subsequent to the effective date of the registration statement. In England the burden of proof that there is a connection between an untrue statement and a decline in the value of a security is upon the plaintiff; in the United States it is the defendant who is expected to show that circumstances having nothing to do with untrue or misleading statements in the registration statement brought about the decline.

CHAPTER V

THE SECURITIES AND EXCHANGE COMMISSION

To the Federal Trade Commission was given the initial responsibility of administering the Securities Act. With the passage in 1934 of legislation for federal regulation of securities exchanges Congress provided for the establishment of a new agency to be known as the Securities and Exchange Commission. With the administration of the Securities Act and the Securities Exchange Act this new Commission was entrusted.[1]

ORGANIZATION OF THE COMMISSION

There are five members of the Securities and Exchange Commission, each of whom is appointed by the President with the advice and consent of the Senate. Unless the appointee is designated to complete the unexpired term of some Commissioner who has resigned, died or been removed, the appointment is for five years. The Commission is organized largely on the divisional basis. The existing divisions are: Registration, Legal, Reorganization, Public Utilities, Trading and Exchange, and Investment Company. In addition there are a chief accountant, a secretary, and an executive staff. During the second year of the life of

---

[1]The Securities and Exchange Commission has been given additional responsibilities since 1934. The most important of these is the administration of the Public Utility Act of 1935. The modification of the bankruptcy law which occurred in 1938 gave the Commission new duties in certain cases involving corporate reorganization. It also administers the Investment Company legislation of 1940.

the Commission a Research Division was established but it was abandoned as a separate division at the end of the fourth year and its work transferred to the Trading and Exchange Division.[2] The main office of the Commission is in Washington, but there are regional offices in New York, Boston, Atlanta, Cleveland, Chicago, Fort Worth, Denver, San Francisco, and Seattle.

The Registration Division

Although the laws of 1933 and 1934 contain statements of the information which corporations are expected to report to the Commission, prescriptions as to the amount of information upon particular items to be required of different classes of organizations and the form in which the information is to be presented in each case are left to the Commission itself. The most basic responsibility of the Registration Division is to make recommendations regarding forms to be used by different classes of registrants, together with the rules and regulations which it thinks ought to apply in the use of these forms. It is also required to provide legal opinions upon specific issues arising as incidents to the application of rules and regulations which happen at any time to be in force.

The work of this unit must of necessity be somewhat experimental. Existing requirements may be burdensome to issuers without providing investors with information commensurate in value with the cost required in getting it; or the information obtained on particular points may be less than intelligent investors need. The Division must be constantly critical of the details of existing forms, rules, and

---

[2] S.E.C., *Fourth Annual Report*, note 8, p. 3. The Protective Committee Study Division ended its hearings in 1936.

regulations. It is required to make inquiries to determine whether they should be modified. It is obliged to make accounting, legal, and economic studies, "for the purpose of developing facts, policies, and customs regarding specific industries to be affected by the promulgation of such rules, regulations, and forms."[3] And whenever changes are contemplated it must confer with accounting and legal organizations, stock exchange officials and others for the purpose of getting advice and of obtaining opinions as to the desirability of the proposed changes.

A second significant duty of the Registration Division is to make an examination of registration statements and prospectuses for the purpose of determining whether they are as complete as the law requires. If, in any case, errors have been made, there are two possible courses of action which this Division may undertake. First, a deficiency letter may be prepared for submission to the registrant advising it of the items which will need to be changed before the statement can be made acceptable. Secondly, if it appears that the registrant has deliberately attempted to lay the groundwork for deceiving investors, immediate opportunity for correction will be withheld provided the Commission can be persuaded to initiate stop order proceedings. Within the Division there are various engineers and valuation experts who render special assistance in testing the validity of registrants' allegations. The Division also holds hearings for "the development of facts and the verification of data submitted in registration statements,"[4] and it conducts hearings in stop order and refusal order cases, advises the Commission in such cases, and if in these proceedings the Commission decides to forbid distribution of any

---

[3]S.E.C., *Second Annual Report*, p. 8.
[4]*Ibid.*, p. 4.

issue of securities the Division prepares orders giving effect to its rulings.

The Legal Division

The first responsibility of the Legal Division is to advise the Commission upon problems of law arising in connection with the enforcement of the various acts which it is required to administer. Similarly it provides the Commission with opinions as to the law regarding particular problems presented in the form of queries submitted by organizations which have filed or are about to file registration statements or prospectuses. If need be, this Division phrases the responses to such inquiries. Certain hearings are conducted by this Division, although hearings involving possible stop orders under the Securities Act are conducted by the Registration Division.[5] If it appears that any of the Acts administered by the Commission are being violated, the Legal Division conducts an investigation. Whenever the Commission is in court, it is represented by this Division. Criminal proceedings are handled by the Department of Justice, but if such cases arise as a consequence of the violation of the laws committed to the administration of the Commission, the Legal Division prepares cases for submission to the Department of Justice or the Post Office Department and renders whatever assistance it is subsequently able to give. The final duty of this Division is to help in the preparation of reports which other divisions may be required to make to Congress.

The Reorganization Division

This Division has the duty of advising the Commission in the discharge of the responsibilities imposed upon it by the

---

[5]The Trading and Exchange Division has charge of hearings upon unlisted trading privileges.

modification in 1938 of the Bankruptcy Act. If a debtor in bankruptcy has indebtedness in excess of three million dollars, the court which has supervision over it is obliged to invite the Securities and Exchange Commission to submit an opinion about such plan or plans as it may choose to submit to the Commission for study.[6] Even though the indebtedness is less than three million dollars the court may call upon the Commission for help if it wishes to do so. The reports of the Commission in all such cases are only advisory, however, for the law permits the court to approve for submission to such stockholders and creditors of the debtor as may be entitled to vote upon it whatever plan conforms, in the judgment of the court, to the standards of fairness set forth in the Act. It is necessary, however, that the report of the Commission or a summary of it be sent to all such persons before they are asked to commit themselves on any plan. Even after the acceptance of a plan as provided by law, the court must give the Securities and Exchange Commission (as well as the Secretary of the Treasury and numerous other persons)[7] an opportunity to be heard before the plan may be declared effective.[8]

The Chief Accountant

The important duty of the chief accountant is to give advice to the Commission upon accounting problems in general and to the accountants who are in the employ of the Commission whenever they are in need of advice or information about accounting problems. It is his duty to assume a supervisory role in dealing with new or unusual problems

[6]Bankruptcy Act, Section 172.
[7]*Ibid.*, Section 179.
[8]The Trading and Exchange Division, the Public Utilities Division, and the Investment Company Division are engaged in activities which are not related to the topic under discussion here.

in accounting, to publish and enforce rules relating to uniform classifications of accounts, to lay down the standards that are to apply when audits or accounting investigations occur. In the formulation of accounting rules and regulations and even in their interpretation he is required by the Commission to consult with members of the staff and with persons not identified with the Commission who are regarded as accounting authorities. Finally, he prepares "accounting briefs, reports and memoranda regarding accounting matters under the jurisdiction of the Commission."[9]

PROBLEMS OF EXEMPTION

Section 3 of the Act enumerates the classes of securities which need not be registered, and Section 4 contains a statement of the transactions which are exempted. The principal classes of exempted securities are:

1. Securities issued or guaranteed by the federal government, by any state or territory or political subdivision thereof, by the District of Columbia, by any public instrumentality of a state or territory of the United States government.
2. Securities issued by the Federal Reserve System or by any bank subject to control by the Federal government or a state government.
3. Notes, drafts, bills of exchange, or bankers acceptances arising out of current transactions "or the proceeds of which have been or are to be used for current transactions" and having a maturity of no more than nine months.
4. Securities of eleemosynary institutions which yield their members no personal profit.
5. Securities of certain building and loan, homestead, farmers cooperative, and savings and loan associations.
6. Securities issued by common carriers subject to the provisions of Section 20a of the Act to Regulate Commerce.
7. Certificates issued by a receiver or trustee in bankruptcy with court approval.

---

[9]S.E.C., *Second Annual Report*, p. 7.

8. Securities exchanged by an issuer for its outstanding securities, claims or property interests "or partly in such exchange and partly in cash" when the persons asked to surrender their claims or property have a right to appear before an appropriate judge or other properly authorized public official to object to the fairness of the proposed exchanges.

9. Securities sold only to persons residing within the state in which the issuer is domiciled.

In addition, the Commission has authority to exempt issues not in excess of $100,000 if it finds that federal supervision is not necessary either for the protection of investors or for the promotion of the public interest.

The exempted transactions are:

1. Transactions by any person who is not an issuer, underwriter or dealer.

2. Transactions by an issuer when there are no public offerings.

3. Transactions by dealers when these transactions do not involve: (a) Sales within one year of the first date the securities were originally issued to the public, or (b) Sales of any portion of an unsold allotment to the dealer.

4. Transactions by brokers when executed through the facilities of exchanges or the over-the-counter market. These transactions are exempted, however, only when they occur on the basis of unsolicited orders by customers. If the broker merely executes orders, initiated by his customers, he "has not induced the sale; his conduct has in no way prejudiced the position of the buyer; he has not assumed the responsibility of using his experience and superior knowledge of the investment to induce the buyer to buy; he has not induced the buyer to rely on his judgment.[10] The advantage of this exemption is that even though a stop order may be in effect individual security holders cannot be prevented from disposing of their securities. Although further distribution must await the lifting of the stop order, transactions resting upon the initiative of owners who are not underwriters or dealers, may continue without interruption.[11]

---

[10]*Brooklyn Manhattan Transit Corporation*, I Decisions 172.

[11]For discussion of the issues in this exemption see House Report 85, 73rd Congress, 1st Session.

The important problems which the Commission has had to consider in dealing with the matter of exemption have related to the administration of those provisions authorizing it to exempt (1) issues of small amounts and (2) transactions which do not involve public offerings.

Exemption of Small Issues

Acting on its authority to exempt issues of no more than $100,000 each, the Commission at an early date waived the requirement of registration for issues that did not exceed $30,000. Until late in 1940, when the Commission modified its rules, exemption of issues of from $30,000 to $100,000 had

"been available only upon varying terms and conditions, such as the compliance with the laws of the states in which the securities were sold, or the use of a prospectus containing certain specified information. Where prospectuses have heretofore been required, they have been examined in the Registration Division of the Commission.

"The new simplified procedure does not require the use of a prospectus in any case. To avail itself of the exemption, a domestic issuer will now need only to send to the nearest Regional Office a letter notifying that office of its intention to sell, together with any selling literature it may plan to use. This letter of notification need contain only such information as the name of the company, the name of the underwriters, the name of the issue to be sold and a brief summary of the intended use of the proceeds. The issuer can give this notice, at its option, either through an informal letter or through the use of a two-page form which will be supplied on request for its convenience. Where the issuer chooses to use a prospectus, the regulation indicates certain skeleton information to be included.

"A broadened exemption is available in several important respects under the new regulation. For example, the Commission takes a new position as to future sales of the securities of the same issuer. Heretofore the Commission's rules have been such that, if the offering was a part of a larger financial program, involving the future sale of additional securities of the same class, the exemption was not available. The new regulation specifically states that the exemption is available even if it is contemplated that after the termination of the offering an offering of additional securities will be made. This will apply in instances, among others, where issuers wish to make annual offerings of already outstanding securities for such purposes as employees' participation plans. In such instances, where the offering is not over $100,000, the exemption will be available.

"Furthermore, the exemption is now available to issuers and their controlling stockholders even though each may wish to offer $100,000 under Regulation A within a single year. Heretofore, in such instances, a registration statement has been necessary.

"The new regulation shifts the Commission's administrative emphasis from the disclosure requirements of the Act to the fraud prevention provisions. The examination procedure which has been followed in the past will be abandoned. The use of a prospectus is no longer required, although any selling literature which is employed must be forwarded to the appropriate Regional Office for its information. The new regulation will be administered from the Regional Offices under the usual supervision from Washington."[12]

Private Offerings

The law exempts private offerings unequivocally. Congress made no effort, however, to establish criteria for distinguishing between public and private offers. It has been necessary, therefore, for the Commission to deal with this hiatus in the law by making periodic pronouncements upon the subject. In 1934 the Securities Division of the Federal Trade Commission, responding to an inquiry about the meaning of the words *public offering*, expressed the very cautious opinion that "an offer made to not more than a small, insignificant number of persons, say twenty-five or so, would not appear to be a 'public offering' within the meaning of the Securities Act."[13] If however, the

---

[12]S.E.C., Securities Act Release No. 2410, December 3, 1940.
[13]Letter to the Corporation Trust Company, April 27, 1934.

securities were obtained with the expectation that they would subsequently be distributed, the transaction could not be regarded as a private sale, no matter how small the number of purchasers. The buyers, by reason of their intention to engage in the distribution of the securities at some time subsequent to the date of the offering to them, would as a consequence of that expectation become underwriters and hence subject to the Act.

Early in 1935 the matter of private offerings had further attention, when the General Counsel of the Commission dealt at considerable length with the problem. The opinion which he expressed was the outgrowth of the Commission's belief that some private financing had probably occurred in violation of the law and that private financing had kept from many investors the opportunity to participate in the purchase of sound issues which had been bought chiefly by institutional investors. Relying upon the earlier opinion, some issuers, not wishing to comply with the Securities Act, had developed the policy of offering their securities to small groups of large investors—chiefly insurance companies—which were in position to declare that their purchases would be made for purposes of investment and hence without any thought of subsequent distribution. It was simple for large institutional buyers to enter into such arrangements. They not only had advisers qualified in matters of investment but they could easily purchase bonds with the expectation of keeping them until maturity.

"In no sense," said the General Counsel, "is the question to be determined exclusively by the number of prospective offerees."

The opinion of the General Counsel is summed up in the following words: "The principal factors to be considered are: 1. The number of offerees and their relationship to each other and to the issuer; 2. The number of units offered; 3. The size of the offering; and 4. The manner of offering. Issuers are also warned of the practical difficulty which purchasers would have in redistributing securities originally issued without registration in reliance on this exemption."[14]

It is not the number of persons who actually buy that is important. Some who do not choose to buy may be approached for the purpose of learning about their interest in a proposed issue. Preliminary conversations and negotiations may transform these persons into offerees even though they never buy. The basis for choosing offerees is likewise important. If they belong to a class which is qualified in getting information of significance to investors, the number of persons to whom offers are made is less significant than if the persons belong to the general public and have no such specialized knowledge. An offer to a limited number of the latter group might be regarded as public, whereas an offer to an identical number of the former group might be classified as private. Moreover, the relationship between the issuer and those to whom its securities are offered must be considered. If the offerees are persons who have direct access to reliable information about the issuer—such as executive officers—the number of offerees necessary to make the offering public would be different from what it would be if other employees who have no such access to information were asked to buy.

If the number of units is large, there is a presumption that the purchaser may contemplate the possibility of subsequent distribution. The same presumption might exist if the number of units actually offered happened to be small but if there existed a provision for conversion of a unit into several units of smaller denomination. It is important,

---

[14]S.E.C., Securities Act Release No. 285, January 24, 1935.

besides, to know whether the issuer is currently offering other securities in the market.

It was the belief of the General Counsel that the exemption of offerings not public in character should apply to none except small issues. It might be expected that others could easily result in public distribution any time after the original transaction had been completed. If securities which are being sold at a private sale are part of an issue which has previously been dealt in on any national securities exchange or in the over-the-counter market, or if there is a likelihood that trading activities of such character may occur at an early date, the right of the issuer to claim exemption should be subject to challenge.

If an issuer resorts to the facilities of underwriters in the distribution of its securities, the evidence is strong that the offering is to be public. If, however, an issuer goes directly to large investors, without utilizing the instrumentalities of public distribution, it may be supposed that the intent is to effect a private sale.

But regardless of the number of offerees, the number of units offered, the size of the offering, or the manner of offering, the position of the dealer may be difficult. If, within a year of the distribution a dealer should buy of the original purchasers any of the securities privately sold, he would be obliged, if he wished to be free from liability under the Securities Act, to satisfy himself that they had been purchased as investments without any thought of later distribution; otherwise he might be subject to all the penalties of the Securities Act in case he should attempt to dispose of the securities. Whether an offering is to be regarded as private or public depends basically, at present, upon the intent of the original purchasers. If the intent is to distribute, the offering is public; if the intent is to retain possession of the securities as investments, the offer is private.

The matter of intent was subjected to a practical test in the case of the Brooklyn Manhattan Transit Corporation.[15] Approximately a year after the Securities Act became effective this corporation issued bonds which were sold to four New York banking houses, each of which was represented on the board of directors of the issuer. All of them promised that, in the distribution of the securities, neither the mails nor any instrumentality of interstate commerce would be employed. Inasmuch as the issuer was a New York corporation and the issue was to be sold in the state of New York, exemption from the requirement of registration was claimed.[16] It was the judgment of the Federal Trade Commission that exemption could not be allowed unless "the securities at the time of completion of ultimate distribution shall be found only in the hands of investors resident within the state."[17] Although this opinion was expressed only a few weeks after the issue was sold to the bankers, nothing was done to persuade the issuer to register under the Securities Act until the Commission decided to deny it the privilege of registering the bonds on a temporary basis under the Securities Exchange Act, thus preventing further sales through the facilities of the New York Stock Exchange. Thereafter the Company, in order to enjoy the benefits of having its bonds listed on the Exchange, registered under the Securities Act. This action was made necessary because the Commission discovered that during the process of distribution some portions of

---

[15]I Decisions 147.

[16]Under Section 5 (c) subsequently repealed. For similar provisions in existing law see Section 3(a)(11).

[17]S.E.C., Securities Act Release No. 201, July 30, 1934.

the issue came into the possession of persons who were not residents of the State of New York.

In support of its original position that the bonds had actually been sold only in intrastate commerce the Company argued that the sale had been completed when the bonds were purchased by the four bankers; that subsequent distribution by them could not be regarded as a violation of the Act by the issuer even though sales were made in other states. If such an argument were tenable, said the Commission, "any issuer might wholly escape from the regulatory provisions of the Act by the simple device of making an original sale of a new security issue to one person residing in the same state as the issuer, followed by immediate interstate distribution by that person."[18] In this case the corporation knew that the securities were to be distributed in violation of the Act, said the Commission, for each of the bankers was represented on the board. The Company should, accordingly, have registered the securities.

The problem of private sales has given the Commission no little concern. The volume has been large and because it has been impossible to differentiate sharply between public and private sales, it may be that in some instances there has been "circumvention . . . of the spirit of the securities law."[19] It is easy, however, to support dissent from this belief by claiming for the Securities Act no other purpose than the protection of investors. Practically all private sales involve institutional investors who are competent to protect themselves without the aid of registration statements and prospectuses. Probably such investors now

[18]*Brooklyn Manhattan Transit Corporation,* I Decisions 161.
[19]T. C. Blaisdell, Director of Monopoly Study for the Securities and Exchange Commission. See *Spectator,* September 15, 1938.

have access to information about certain issuers which, without the Securities Act, they might not be able to get. Not only is this true of certain issuers that actually register their securities; it is likely that institutional investors are able as a preliminary to a private purchase to obtain information that would not otherwise be available to them because the issuer knows that failure to sell privately will necessitate registration if public distribution must occur, and hence may be more ready to give information about itself than it would be willing to give in the absence of such a contingency. But whether this be true or not, the institutional investor is skilled in the art of investment and needs but little of the help of the Securities and Exchange Commission in getting information about issuers.

It may possibly be that protection of investors will come to have a meaning different from the consensus of opinion regarding it which apparently prevailed in Congress at the time the Securities Act was passed. Investors were to be protected merely by giving them access to certain varieties of information which would help them to judge the merits of opportunities for participating in the affairs of particular issuers. When the Commission expresses concern over the fact that private offerings, being ordinarily high grade securities, deprive investors in general of investment opportunities, it gives to the Securities Act an interpretation which Congress probably did not intend. It is nevertheless ironical that the very legislation which was meant to protect investors has deprived some of them of excellent investment opportunities. It has been particularly repressive in the case of small institutional buyers which have not been asked to participate in purchases of high grade issues of large corporations and of many individual investors who have been obliged to surrender excellent bonds merely because the issuer, very properly taking advantage of lower interest rates, saw fit to sell its refunding bonds at a private sale.

It has been argued that securities purchased at private sales lose their marketability unless they are subsequently registered. This contention is not wholly valid, for the General Counsel of the Commission has expressed the opinion that "if the securities in question were in fact purchased by the initial purchaser for investment rather than for resale, dealers' sales thereof to the public would not necessitate registration under the Securities Act."[20] Should this continue to express the views of the Commission and should the courts accept such an attitude, it would obviously be very difficult for anybody to disprove the claim of a well advised institutional investor that its purpose at the time of the original purchase was to retain ownership of the securities as a permanent investment.

Investment banks have felt the impact of private sales in a significant way. Since the Securities Act became effective, sales of corporate securities have been of no great magnitude. Investment bankers would still have done but a fraction of the business they did during a period of similar length prior to 1933 had they been able to add to issues actually originated all those issues which have been sold privately since the Securities Act became effective. The issues sold privately could, for the most part, have been sold by investment bankers with but little sales resistance. The bankers have thus been deprived of an important source of income, and some of them feel that issuers have weakened their future financial position both because they have foregone the advice which bankers could have given

---

[20] S.E.C., Securities Act Release No. 603, December 16, 1935.

them and because bankers may not in the future be disposed to participate in public distribution of new issues of their securities. Proponents of private sales allege, however, that large institutional investors are in position to give sound financial advice and that because of the reputation such purchasers have for conservatism in buying securities, issuers, able to dispose of issues at private sales, so enhance their financial reputation that public distribution of future issues may possibly be made easier.

There is another objection to private sales which at present does not appear to be important but which may become significant in the future. The issuer cannot easily take advantage of low prices of its own bonds to retire them when the bonds have been sold privately. If the long term interest rate should rise significantly, it can be expected that publicly distributed securities which have been sold recently to take advantage of low interest rates, will be available at much lower prices than prevailed at the time of distribution. If there is an organized market for such securities, the issuer may find it advantageous to use some of its resources to reduce its debt through open market purchases. Unless the purchaser at a private sale is disposed to sell at a loss in principal, there can be no such opportunity for the issuer to retire its privately placed bonds in this manner.

There are, however, many immediate advantages of private sales. There are numerous expenses from which the corporation is relieved. There are no registration fees; in many cases there are no underwriters to be paid; there are no fees to be paid stock exchanges for listing the securities; there are no newspaper advertisements for forthcoming redemptions; attorney fees, cost of printing and expense involved in transfers are less. Not only is there saving in these and other expenses, but the issuer may be less handicapped in making future modifications in its trust indentures, should that become necessary or advisable, if it has to negotiate with only a few large investors than if it must get the consent of thousands of widely scattered persons, some of whom are unknown to the issuer.

FORMS AND PROSPECTUSES

The Commission has authority "to prescribe the form or forms in which required information shall be set forth."[21] It also has power to permit the omission of such items of information as Schedule A calls for if it finds that these are not necessary "in respect of any class of issuers or securities;" it can demand items of information other than those specified in Schedule A if "necessary or appropriate in the public interest or for the protection of investors."[22] The success of the Securities Act must inevitably rest, in a very important way, upon the attitude which the Commission takes toward the character of reporting required of issuers. It was recognized by the Director of the Forms and Regulations Division in 1937 that the amount of information which may be assembled is not necessarily all that an investor should have in order to judge the quality of a registered security. The investor ought to be informed about the general economic situation, and he should recognize that there "are intangibles which, to a very considerable degree, may have influence upon the worth of an issue, but which cannot properly be made the subject of full inquiry by a general questioning, as being too elusive in character."[23]

---

[21]Section 19(a).
[22]*Ibid.*, Section 7.
[23]Comment of H. H. Neff in *Journal of Business*, University of Iowa, March, 1937.

The basic problem of the Commission has been to provide investors with as large an amount of useful information about each individual issue as is consistent with the resources which it has for eliciting such information. The ideal plan would probably be to deal with each registration statement as a separate problem, but that would be impractical. Because of the impractability of an individualized approach, the Commission has been obliged to choose between identical treatment for all and classification of registrants. Whichever of these two methods may be employed, there must certainly be redundancy of material in some statements and inadequacy in others. Although it is impossible, when the approach is generalized, for the Commission to overcome these handicaps, less difficulty is encountered when it resorts to classification.

This principle is exemplified in the history of Forms A-1 and A-2. Form A-1, being the earlier, was to be used by corporations with a record of successful experience, as well as by those that had no record or that had had a record wholly unsatisfactory from the financial point of view. It soon became evident that the varieties of information necessary for an evaluation of the securities of seasoned corporations is far from identical with that which an investor needs when he is attempting to judge the prospect of a promotional undertaking. Following the publication of Form A-1 the Securities Exchange Act became effective. As an incident in the administration of this law the Commission published Form 10 which was to be used for the registration of securities that had been listed on national securities exchanges. The form was the result of extensive study by the Commission in cooperation with many experts, particularly committees of the American Institute of Accountants, the New York State Society of Certified Public

Accountants, and the American Society of Certified Public Accountants. Early in January, 1935, the Commission published Form A-2 to be used in registrations under the Securities Act by "any corporation which files profit and loss statements for three years and which meets either one of the following conditions: (a) such corporation has made annually available to its security holders, for at least ten years, financial reports . . . including at least a balance sheet and a profit and loss or income statement or (b) such corporation had a net income for any two fiscal years . . . preceding the date of the latest balance sheet filed with the registration statement."[24]

Form 10 was designed to obtain information about corporations with a history, for it was they and they alone that had securities listed on reputable securities exchanges. It is easy to suppose that any differentiation the Commission might wish to make between seasoned and promotional organizations in the administration of the Securities Act would begin by application to seasoned corporations of treatment similar to that used in the administration of the Act of 1934. And that is exactly what happened. Form A-2 was based upon Form 10.[25]

Commenting upon Form 10 the Commission said: "The outstanding advances which these requirements represent over reporting practices already in vogue are first, a greater emphasis upon the accounting steps involved in income determination, and second, a more complete explanation of the changes which have occurred in balance sheet items during the year under report. It is in these matters that the information of greatest moment to investors is to

---

[24]Instruction Book for Form A-2.

[25]The accounting requirements of the two are almost identical except that Form A-2 calls for profit and loss statements for three years whereas Form 10 asks for a report for one year only.

be found. The requirements give less attention, on the other hand, to historical information concerning the company, since all companies affected are already listed on the exchanges and have been reporting consistently under existing exchange requirements. Nevertheless, in addition to financial statements for the current year, leading questions are asked regarding the accounting practices of the company during the last ten years, designed to bring out such major adjustments as may have occurred in principal balance sheet items.''[26]

Whereas Form A-1 places a great deal of emphasis upon the organizational history of the registrant and, particularly its relationships with promoters, Form A-2 probes deeply for information about earnings experience. If there have been any exceptional entries since 1922 which might distort the history of its experience, such entries must be revealed. Information is required, too, with respect to policy in computing depreciation charges. The relationships with subsidiaries must be presented in such a way as to eliminate distortions that might arise from intercompany accounts. For example, intercompany sales must be eliminated; so must intercompany profits unless there is good reason for not doing so. Form A-2 gives greater recognition to the importance of material contracts than is to be found in Form A-1. The latter form merely asks for information about material contracts not made in the ordinary course of business,[27] and then in a footnote presents without comment a quotation from the law as to certain types of contracts which are to be regarded as being material. The Instruction Book for Form A-2, on the other hand, deals with the problem of material contracts much

---

[26]S.E.C., Securities Exchange Act Release No. 66, December 21, 1934.
[27]Item 46.

more explicitly. "If the contract is such as ordinarily accompanies the kind of business conducted by the registrant, it is made in the ordinary course of business unless the amount of the subject matter of the contract in proportion to the total assets and volume of business of the registrant and its subsidiaries, the duration of the contract and the party with whom contracted are such as to make it of an extraordinary nature."[28] If they do not involve directors, officers, promoters, affiliates, the following are not material contracts: (1) Any contract for service or employment which does not require an outlay of more than one per cent of total selling, general and administrative expenses; (2) Any contract for the purchase or sale of fixed assets which will not involve payments in excess of three per cent of the value of all fixed assets less valuation reserves; (3) Any contract for the purchase or sale of current assets if the amount of the transaction is no more than three per cent of the net sales as shown by the latest annual profit and loss statement; (4) Any contract of indebtedness not in excess of three per cent of the net worth of the registrant.

Regarding contracts involving outlays in excess of the percentages which have just been enumerated, the Commission refuses to speak with finality. By implication, however, contracts which do not fall within the limits specified are to be regarded as material and in any case, no matter how small the amount involved, the following invariably possess the quality of materiality:

(1) "Any management contract or contract providing for special bonuses or profit sharing arrangements except the following: (a) Ordinary purchase and sales agency agreements; (b) Payments made to security holders as such; (c) Labor bonuses; (d) Salesmen's bonuses; (e) Agreements with managers of stores in a chain store organization or similar organization.

---

[28]Instruction Book Form A-2, Item 41.

(2) Every contract by or with a public utility company or an affiliate thereof providing for the giving or receiving of technical or financial advice or service, (if such contract may involve a charge to any party thereto at a rate in excess of $2,500 per year in cash or securities or anything else of value)."[29]

Having differentiated between seasoned and unseasoned issuers, the Commission has further classified the latter group of registrants. In December, 1936, it published Form A-O-1 for the use of mining companies without any history. They are not asked for balance sheets or profit and loss statements, but instead report upon cash receipts and disbursements. Emphasis is placed upon such items as prices paid by promoters for property which they sell to the registrant, bases used in valuing property, and costs of distributing securities.

The Commission has not only differentiated among issuers on the basis of their history; it has differentiated among them on the basis of variations in the types of activity in which they engage. There are, for instance, special forms for various classes of certificates of deposit, voting trust certificates, securities in reorganization, fractional undivided oil and gas royalty interests, securities of unincorporated investment trusts, and corporate bonds secured by mortgage insured by the Federal Housing Administration.[30] In addition there are several forms for use in making annual reports under the Securities Exchange Act which certain issuers must now agree to make as a condition for qualifying their registration statements.[31]

The problem of reporting is in the experimental stage and will probably continue to remain there as long as the prevailing policy with respect to social control over security

---

[29]*Ibid.*
[30]These are the titles used by the Commission.
[31]Securities Exchange Act, Section 15(d).

issuance persists.   There will always be questions as to the sufficiency or redundancy of some of the data called for. Such will continue to be the result, in part, of inability to classify issuers in such a way as to avoid calling for data of inconsequential importance from certain issuers without omitting, coincidentally, requests for highly important information from others; it will be the result, in part, of the inability of any commission, no matter what its approach to omniscience, to know precisely what information to call for.   In its entire experience, for example, the Commission has failed to find ways for meeting the registration problems of insurance companies, promotion companies (with the possible exception of those using Form A-O-1), companies recently reorganized through mergers, consolidations, and insolvency, as well as the sale of securities offered in secondary distributions.[32]

Prospectuses[33]

It is illegal to sell a registered security without giving each purchaser a prospectus which meets the requirements of the law.   A "notice, circular, advertisement, letter, or communication in respect of a security" is a prospectus unless it merely "states from whom a written prospectus . . . may be obtained and in addition, does no more than identify the security, state the price thereof, and state by whom orders will be executed."[34]   But "it must be borne in mind that a prospectus is a selling medium,"[35] which is used only after a registration statement has become effec-

---

[32]See article on forms by H. H. Neff, director of the Forms and Registration Division of the Securities and Exchange Commission, 51 *Harvard Law Review* 1354 (1938).

[33]For definition of prospectus see page 60.

[34]Securities Act, Section 2(10).

[35]S.E.C., Securities Act Release No. 464, August 19, 1935.

tive. During the waiting period the Commission has allowed registrants to distribute ''circulars, describing a security in the method in which a prospectus conforming to Section 10 describes a security but clearly and unmistakably marked to indicate that they are informative only, negativing without equivocation either impliedly or expressly any intent to solicit offers to buy or to make an offer to sell.''[36] This attitude toward publicity during the waiting period was supported by the belief that one of the important purposes of the waiting period was to provide investors with an opportunity to acquaint themselves with information needed for satisfactory evaluation of investment opportunities. Anything that an underwriter might do, prior to the effective date of a registration statement, to help educate the investor was to be regarded as consonant with the law, provided the information circulated did not exceed that permitted in a prospectus and could not be construed as an offer to sell or as a solicitation of the patronage of prospective buyers.[37]

Further clarification of the law occurred almost two years later when the General Counsel was asked for an opinion as to the legal position of a statistical service which summarized certain information it had as to forthcoming issues and gave them investment ratings.[38] The summaries and ratings it published in its bulletins which it not only sent to its subscribers but which it was prepared to sell in as large quantity as desired to any person interested in buy-

---

[36]Opinion of the General Counsel, S.E.C., Securities Act Release No. 70, November 6, 1933.

[37]See also House Report 85, 73rd Congress, 1st Session: ''It is, therefore, possible for underwriters who wish to inform a selling group or dealers generally of the nature of a security that will be offered for sale after the effective date of a registration statement, to circularize among them full information respecting such a security.''

[38]S.E.C., Securities Act Release No. 464, August 19, 1935.

ing. For its summarizations and rating, however, it received no compensation from any issuer, underwriter, or dealer. Two problems arose from this situation: was it legal to distribute these bulletins during the waiting period, and would they be regarded as prospectuses if distributed after a registration statement became effective? The General Counsel was of the opinion that no provision of the Securities Act would be violated by circulating these bulletins during the waiting period, but that an underwriter or dealer might become liable for using them after a statement had become effective unless they should be sent by such a distributor only to those persons previously provided with legal prospectuses. Whether such liability exists in any case would probably depend upon the character of the use to which such bulletins might be put.

"If an underwriter or dealer were to supplement a bulletin with selling literature or with a recommendation to the recipient as to the desirability of purchase, or were to attempt to obtain from the recipient some indication of interest however tentative, in purchasing the described security, such action in my opinion, would almost conclusvely establish that the bulletin was being used in an attempt to dispose of or to solicit an order for the purchase of the security."[39]

The following year a prospective underwriter asked the Commission for a ruling as to whether it would be permitted to summarize certain information in the registration statement and distribute it during the waiting period. The answer, presented by the General Counsel, was that if the "summary contains no recommendation or opinion as to the merits of the security, is a fair summarization of the salient information contained in the registration statement, and does not stress or in any way emphasize the favorable as

---

[39]*Ibid.*

against the unfavorable aspects of such security'' and if the form used is appropriate, the distribution of it during the waiting period cannot be regarded as illegal.[40]

The prospectus is the sole source of information to the average investor and unless he chooses to go to Washington or gets photostatic copies of registration statements[41] or obtains information from those who do examine these statements, he must rely upon the prospectus which in an important sense, is the keystone of the Securities Act. It is, to be sure, based upon the registration statement, but without it the Securities Act would be of no immediate significance to most investors except insofar as it provides the legal basis for rescission of sales and claims for damages.

No longer is it possible for issuers or underwriters to determine what may be included in the prospectus; no longer is it possible to accent hope and slight past experience. It is the prerogative of the Commission to dictate what the content shall be. The law[42] says that with certain minor exceptions it ''shall contain the same statements made in the registration statement'' but it authorizes the Commission to allow the omission of any items or the inclusion of others if in the exercise of its discretion it believes such to be ''necessary or appropriate in the public interest or for the protection of investors.''

Although issuers and underwriters are now wholly subject to the will of the Commission in the preparation of prospectuses, a new and very difficult problem has arisen. How is the Commission to provide the investor with information which will be at once adequate and helpful? A prospectus can easily become so voluminous that the average

---

[40]S.E.C., Securities Act Release No. 802, May 24, 1936.
[41]See Rule 121 for information about charges for such copies.
[42]Section 10.

investor is not only discouraged with its size but could hardly understand its content even though he might have the courage to attempt its mastery. The Commission has wrestled with this problem first by permitting the omission of certain information required in registration statements,[43] and secondly, by encouraging simplification in the presentation of required material. Although the prospectus must be accurate both as to detail and as a whole, and as complete as the Commission chooses, unnecessary prolixity is regarded as undesirable.

STANDARDS OF TRUTHFULNESS

The Commission may keep a statement from becoming effective if it is "incomplete or inaccurate in any material respect" or issue a stop order if the statement, having become effective, "includes any untrue statement of a material fact or omits to state any material fact required to be stated therein or necessary to make the statement therein not misleading." The Commission is thus obliged to restrict its objections to items in registration statements which have deficiencies possessing the quality of materiality. Although of basic importance, the word *material* is not defined in the Act and hence the Commission has been obliged to formulate a definition of its own. Following the British precedent in dealing with the problem of materiality the Federal Trade Commission in an early opinion defined a material fact as one "which if it had been correctly stated or disclosed would have deterred or tended to deter the average prudent investor from purchasing the securities in question."[44] Although the Commission has no authority to

---

[43]For statements of items that may be omitted see General Rules and Regulations beginning with Rule 830, and the Instruction Book for Form A-2.

[44]*Charles A. Howard et al.* I Decisions 8.

interfere with the sale of securities unless a material fact has been omitted or incorrectly stated, it has nevertheless taken the position that if a statement is materially incorrect, it may challenge the accuracy of other statements even when they involve no question of materiality.[45]

Standards of Truthfulness for Voluntary Information

If a registrant chooses to include in its registration statement information which it is under no obligation to report, that information must be accurate. The Commission has ruled that if a statement not called for is false, the consequence may possibly be a material misstatement which would justify the issuance of a stop order.[46] Moreover, "the inclusion in the prospectus of information not strictly applicable to the matters in hand may be misleading unless the extent to which this information is applicable and relevant is made clearly explicit."[47] This opinion was the result of the inclusion in the registrant's prospectus of a quotation from a professional paper of the United States Geological Survey regarding "three determinations of the fineness of bullion obtained by amalgamation." There was no reference to the fact that this statement related to a mine which belonged to another organization. Inasmuch as no effort was made to show the applicability of the statement to property owned by the registrant, the inclusion of the quotation was held to be misleading.[48]

[45]As a matter of procedure the Commission never defends its judgment that a fact is material unless the respondent raises a question about it. A claim that any fact is material will be assumed to be so in the absence of any claim to the contrary by the registrant. The Mutual Industrial Bankers, Inc., questioned the materiality of certain deficiencies. The objections were brushed aside, however, by categorical denial of the registrant's claims. I Decisions 272.
[46]*Unity Gold Corporation.* I Decisions 28.
[47]*Gilpin Eureka Consolidated Mines, Inc.* I Decisions 761.
[48]See also *American Tung Grove Developments, Inc.*, S.E.C., Securities Act Release No. 2361, Sept. 30, 1940.

Omissions

This same registrant put in its prospectus a statement based upon findings of the Geological Survey regarding the average amounts of gold and silver in certain lots of ore obtained from its own mines over a period of years. Although it did not give the Geological Survey credit for the findings, the report in the prospectus was correct as far as it went. It failed, however, to include any statement as to the zinc content of these ores, and that would be important to those informed upon the technical problems of gold mining, for the presence of zinc complicates the processing of gold ore. The Commission objected to that part of the prospectus to which reference has just been made both because the registrant, through the process of editing an authoritative report, omitted vital information, and because, by omitting reference to the source of its data, it deprived inquisitive investors of "avenues to further information."

The Snow Point Mining Company[49] reported in detail in its registration statement how it expected to use the proceeds to be obtained from the sale of its securities. It appeared to be planning "facilities suitable to, and adequate for, a large mining operation."[50] Although it described these proposed facilities with meticulous care, it neglected to provide an appropriate "description of the mining property itself." This property was known to have occasional small but rich pockets together with great stretches in which no ore was to be found at all. The Commission felt that unless investors were given information as to these characteristics of the mining property they could have no way of judging the hazards with which the mining venture would be confronted.

---

[49] I Decisions 311.
[50] *Ibid.*, p. 316.

Charles A. Howard and others, acting as a protective committee, reported to the Commission that it knew of no rival committee. When this statement was challenged, the registrant replied that although it knew of a rival group, the rival could have no legal right to issue certificates of deposit until its registration statement should become effective at some uncertain time in the future, and that until its registration statement did become effective, the rival committee could not be regarded as having a legal existence. Objecting to this reasoning, the Commission remarked that the "half truth embodied in the registrant's answer is the very type of untruth to which the language of the Securities Act relating to omissions of material fact has reference."[51]

The Golden Conqueror Mines[52] thought investors would be interested to know that its president and manager had put two other mining companies on a dividend paying basis. Many investors are not familiar with the very common practice employed by corporations engaged in the exploitation of wasting assets, of paying dividends out of capital. Although the two companies which had been managed by the registrant's president had actually paid dividends, the Commission discovered that they had been operated at a loss and that the registration statement, by omitting reference to this fact, was untrue.

Misstatements and Corrections

A registrant cannot justify misstatements of particular items by alleging that when an entire statement is read a correct impression may be obtained. The Continental Distillers and Importers Corporation[53] presented an appraisal

---

[51]*Charles A. Howard et al.* I Decisions 11.
[52]II Decisions 642.
[53]I Decisions 54.

of its properties which the appraisal company declared to be true when read as a whole even though particular portions of it could not be regarded as "statements of present facts." From this view the Commission dissented by asserting that "no amount of flat contradiction elsewhere in the report could avoid the effect of direct false statements such as the statements that buildings existed which did not, that buildings had been remodeled and specially constructed for distilling purposes when they had not, and that there was a driven well when there was not."[54]

Literal Truth Not Enough

The Commission believes that each individual item may be accurate but that the total impression may be such as to make the statement as a whole untrue. This is more likely to be the case with prospectuses than with registration statements both because it is proper for registrants to omit certain items from prospectuses and more particularly because they have some freedom in arranging the sequence of data. "In several instances," said the Commission, "we have found that the statutory standard has been violated through artful arrangement of presentation, notwithstanding all the essential facts have been presented at some point or another within a prospectus."[55]

The Mind of the Investor

It is impossible to disregard the mind of the investor in considering standards of truthfulness. The expert engineer or accountant or financial analyst may not be deceived by a statement or prospectus, but if the average investor is

---

[54]*Ibid.*, p. 80.
[55]*Income Estates of America, Inc.* II Decisions 442.

likely to be deceived, a refusal or stop order is appropriate. That appeals which are directed toward a special class of potential investors who are untrained in the "niceties of finance and investment" should be accompanied by frankness was emphasized by the Commission in the National Educators Mutual Association case.[56] This belief that adequate disclosure requires consideration for the investment ability of any special group among whose number the issuer expects its securities to be distributed was reiterated in the case of Income Estates of America, Inc.[57] "Inherent complexity of the proposition presented no less than the fact that the proposition is to be presented to the financially uninitiate, thus increasing the danger of confusion, should operate to increase the degree of frankness necessary in the prospectus."[58]

There are many ways of deceiving the uninitiated investor. One of them is the use of "meaningless, high sounding and pseudoscientific phrases designed principally to impress the uninformed." The Franco Mining Corporation[59] had included in its registration statement a lengthy discussion of the geological features of its property. "Massive tufaceous, andesitic and ryolitic of various thickness also form a part of the Devonian formation."[60] Condemning the unintelligibility of such statements as this but nevertheles admitting the necessity of genuine scientific phraseology, the Commission wondered whether such language as the registrant had used had any other purpose than "to impress the uninformed."

But there are circumstances under which a correctly used scientific expression may create a false impression upon the

---

[56] I Decisions 216.
[57] II Decisions 445.
[58] *Ibid.*, 445.
[59] I Decisions 292.
[60] *Ibid.*, 291.

minds of some investors.   In the Rickard Ramore Gold Mines, Ltd., case the Commission said that "the prospectus was intended to be circulated, not among mining engineers, but among the general investing public.   There is nothing in the prospectus to inform the public that the word 'indicated' was used as a word of art to express the fact that there is at most only a probability of the presence of an ore body.   To the laymen the phrases 'indicated ore' and 'indicated ore body' are suggestive of the positive presence of ore.' "[61]

Nor may truth be obscured by emphasis or the lack of it which diverts the mind of the investor.   The use of bold type for the one and fine print for the other has had a long and unsavory history in the experience of those who have endeavored to deceive.   The Bankers Union Life Company printed on the first page of its endowment bond in black and red the statement *"Amount $1000"* and on the back *"Face Amount $1000."*   In small type it explained that at the maturity of the endowment bond the Company would pay $750 in cash and five shares of stock *"herein valued at Fifty Dollars ($50.00) per share."*   To this statement the Commission objected, first because of its unyielding opinion that no amount of fine print can destroy legally an incorrect impression covered by statements in bold type when standing alone; and secondly, because the expression "herein valued at Fifty Dollars" created an impression of value which did not as a matter of fact exist because the valuation was purely nominal.

More Than Good Faith Required

The purpose of the Securities Act is to protect investors by giving them reliable information.   Although many is-

---

[61] II Decisions 388.

suers have been deliberately dishonest, occasionally there is one which is honest but wholly incompetent and hence unable to give an accurate account of itself. Such was the Herman Hanson Oil Syndicate.[62] Admitting that the registration statement was not the result, necessarily, of an intent to deceive, the Commission nevertheless felt that the "Act of 1933 requires more than good faith; it requires, as well, that those who seek the trusteeship of the public's money on the basis of information in the registration statement and the prospectus, must live up to certain minimum standards of ability and due care in their preparation. It will not suffice that a registrant has attempted to prepare a registration statement to the best of its ability. It is necessary that it meet the standards imposed by the law."[63]

Inferences

The Commission believed that it was the purpose of Gold Hunter Extension, Inc.,[64] to trade upon the name of the Gold Hunter Mine. The prospectus emphasized "the geographical proximity of the registrant's properties to the Gold Hunter Mine." No effort was made in the registration statement or prospectus to indicate to investors the need of distinguishing between the two organizations. Largely because of the method which it used in advertising its name the registrant was forbidden to continue with the distribution of its securities. The Commission could have allowed the matter to stand without comment upon whether it would have raised any question had there been adequate publicity designed to prevent investors from being confused about the registrant's name. Instead it issued what

---

[62]II Decisions 743.
[63]*Ibid.*, 746.
[64]III Decisions 891.

might be regarded as a warning by saying that "it is not necessary for the Commission to decide whether it could properly suspend the effectiveness of a registration statement even were the name accompanied by an explanatory statement."

Time as a Factor in Truth

The Commission has no power to interfere with the sale of a security by means of a stop order if the registration statement accurately portrays the truth about the issue as of the day when it became effective. If material changes occur in the position of the issuer between the filing of a statement and the end of the waiting period, the Commission has authority to require modification of the statement, notwithstanding the fact that the statement was true when it was filed. On the other hand, the Commission has no power to interfere with the sale of securities if material changes in the position of the issuer take place after the effective date of the statement.[65]

In some cases, however, it is impossible for the Commission to be sure of the validity of any item of information as of the time when the registration statement became effective. There are two aspects of this circumstance, only one of which is important at this point. The Commission may have allowed a faulty statement to become effective merely because it was unable for want of resources or because of the inability of its staff to make adequate inquiry; or, and this is of significance here, it may be that the truth in a registration statement can be revealed only through the experience of the registrant subsequent to the effective date of its registration statement. An issuer may allege, for example, that it intends to use the proceeds of an issue for

---

[65]*Charles A. Howard et al.* I Decisions 10.

the purpose of investing in the securities of other organizations. It is impossible for anybody not identified with the issuer to know when its statement becomes effective whether it intends to diversify its investments or increase its interest in other organizations which it or its officers or principal stockholders wish to control. The matter of intent can be dealt with satisfactorily only after the issuer has had opportunity to make commitments. The Commission, without departing from the conception that the registration statement must tell the truth as of the date of its effectiveness, has nevertheless resorted to the expedient of testing the accuracy of statements regarding intent as of the day when it became effective, by inquiring into conduct subsequent to the date of effectiveness of the statement.[66]

PROCEDURE

Each registrant is required to pay a filing fee of one one-hundredth of one per cent of the total sum for which its securities are to be offered.[67] When this fee is paid, its statement, filed in triplicate, is stamped with the date of receipt and is given a docket number. The purpose of the former is to establish a date for determining when the statement will become effective in the absence of any deficiency whose correction may require postponement of effectiveness beyond the waiting period. The purpose of the docket number is to facilitate the physical handling of the statement by providing a place for it in the files and a basis for recording movements of it throughout the offices of the Commission.

As soon as possible after the receipt of any statement it is turned over to the Registration Division for examination.

---

[66]See, *e.g.*, II Decisions 669 and 726.
[67]In no case may the fee be less than twenty-five dollars.

At the head of this division there is a director who has immediate supervision over several assistant directors, three of whom specialize in registrations arising from the requirement of the Securities Act. One of these three assistant directors is concerned with elucidation of rules and regulations under the Securities Act both for the benefit of the Commission and private citizens or organizations, including registrants. The other two assistant directors devote themselves primarily to the work of examining registration statements. Under their supervision there are five examining groups, each of which is headed by a senior analyst. Under his control there are seven or eight persons consisting in each group of an attorney, an accountant and five or six examiners. When a senior analyst receives the three copies of a statement, he gives one of them to the attorney, another to the accountant, and the third to an examiner. The attorney is interested in legal problems, such as opinions which are expressed by counsel for the registrant or its underwriters, legality of contracts, options and other agreements. If there is, in his judgment, any deficiency, he will make a memorandum of it. The accountant makes an examination of the balance sheet, of profit and loss statements, of footnotes, of supporting schedules, of the accountant's certificate, of the accounting procedures that have been employed. If he observes any deficiencies, he, too, prepares a memorandum. The examiner studies the history of the organization, its management, the reasons for the issue and general accounting and legal matters. He, likewise, prepares a report of any deficiencies which, in his opinion, ought to be corrected. After the three have completed their examinations, they meet with the senior analyst and together the alleged deficiencies are considered. If it appears, at the close of this discussion, that there are genuine deficiencies, the group prepares a deficiency letter which is sent to the Assistant Director in charge of the group. Unless special problems have been presented, the Assistant Director, if he pleases, then sends to the registrant a letter indicating the items which are in need of correction before the statement may become effective. The Assistant Director is under no obligation to accept the group report, however. On his own initiative and without further consultation he may modify or reject the report. If, however, new problems of accounting arise, the Supervising Accountant of the Registration Division is asked for advice. If the Supervising Accountant and the group accountant are in disagreement, the issue is presented to the Chief Accountant for an opinion. In cases involving problems upon which rules have not yet been formulated, the director of the division may be asked for an opinion. If it is a problem of policy, the director may ask the Commission itself for a ruling.

Amendments

Amendments to registration statements occur either on the initiative of registrants or in response to deficiency letters. Correspondence between the Commission and registrants which relates to deficiencies is confidential so far as the Commission is concerned. In the absence of formal dissent by a registrant, there is ordinarily no way of knowing except by inference based upon an examination of amendments to individual statements just how the Commission has handled particular deficiency problems.[68] The Commission has discretion to decide whether amendments may postpone the effective date of the registration statement.

---

[68] B. B. Greidinger used this method in getting material for his book on *Accounting Requirements of the Securities and Exchange Commission.*

Unless it authorizes acceleration of the effectiveness of amendments they can become effective, even when acceptable to the Commission, only after the expiration of twenty days.[69]

The effectiveness of many statements has been accelerated but in other cases the Commission has been less generous. The Callahan Zinc-Lead Company[70] filed a registration statement in the summer of 1934 which it amended from time to time under circumstances preventing the statement from becoming effective. In the latter part of March, 1935, another amendment was filed and with it a request that the statement be made effective at once in order that the registrant might proceed with immediate distribution of its securities. The Commission had made an investigation of the company, however, and had succeeded in getting information which the registrant had not known itself. "It seems to us that stockholders quite reasonably might expect that their directors would learn all the pertinent facts concerning properties before binding their company to purchase them. . . . But there is no good reason why we should advance the date when this registration should become effective and when the registrant may begin to sell this stock to its present stockholders for whose interests and

---

[69]Securities Act, Rule 945. "A registrant desiring the Commission's consent to the filing of an amendment with the effect provided in Section 8 (a) of the Act may apply for such consent at or before the time of filing the amendment. The application shall be signed by the registrant and shall state fully the grounds upon which made. The Commission's consent shall be deemed to have been given and the amendment shall be treated as part of the registration statement upon the entry of an order to that effect." Rule 946: "An amendment made prior to the effective date of the registration statement shall be deemed to have been made pursuant to an order of the Commission within the meaning of Section 8 (a) of the Act so as to be treated as part of the registration statement only when the Commission shall after the filing of such amendment find that it has been filed pursuant to its order."

[70]I Decisions 115.

protection it has acted in this matter with so little caution."[71]

If a registrant does not make corrections in accordance with the wishes of the Commission, it runs the risk of stop order proceedings, but even though stop order proceedings are pending, the Commission will drop the charges if satisfactory amendments are filed before the case comes to trial, and may even allow the statement to become effective at once. This is what happened in the case of the Equity Corporation.[72] Although the activities of this corporation had been of such a character that the Commission felt inspired to make a lengthy statement about them, it nevertheless accepted the amendments as curing the deficiencies. It has no choice in such cases about allowing a statement to become effective, but it could have required a delay of twenty days after the last amendment was filed before the sale of securities might occur. In spite of its criticism of the failure of the company to be frank in its original statements, the Commission was nevertheless unwilling to penalize it by insisting upon a waiting period to make the amendments effective. If amendments are filed after oral argument in stop order proceedings, the Commission is under no obligation, it has ruled,[73] to consider these amendments in deciding whether a stop order should be issued.

The circumstances of each case are decisive when the Commission considers the question of acceleration. It explained in its published opinion in the matter of the Consolidated Funds Corporation[74] just why it allowed the

---

[71]*Ibid.*, 119 and 120.
[72]II Decisions 675.
[73]*Petersen Engine Company, Inc.* II Decisions 893.
[74]II Decisions 724.

amendments to become effective at once. Not only did the amendments correct the deficiencies, and hence require discontinuance of stop order proceedings, but there were special circumstances which justified acceleration of effectiveness of the amendments. The company had made no sale of its securities for approximately two years and it promised to send copies of the amendments to all its stockholders provided the Commission allowed them to become effective immediately.

The Queensboro Gold Mines, Ltd.,[75] had from time to time requested the Commission to postpone the effective date of its statement in order that it might file amendments.[76] The Act requires the filing of a 90-day balance sheet and this the Commission decided the registrant would have to do in order to qualify its securities for sale.[77] The repeated requests for postponement had made the balance sheet it submitted too old to satisfy the standard set forth in the act. The registrant was accordingly instructed to file the required amendment before proceeding with the distribution of its securities.

Withdrawals

Some registrants which have been unwilling to comply with the wishes of the Commission regarding deficiencies have dealt with the problem by withdrawing their statements and foregoing the distribution of their securities. The right to withdraw, however, is not unqualified. The policy of the Commission is to allow withdrawals if "consistent

---

[75]II Decisions 860.
[76]In accordance with Rule 943.
[77]There were other corrections to be made, but they are unimportant in this portion of the discussion.

with the public interest and the protection of investors.''[78] If the registrant wishes to withdraw before a statement becomes effective, there is no way by which the Commission can prevent it. The constitutional right of a registrant to withdraw, if the statement is not effective, was established in the Jones case.[79] The day before the end of the waiting period an order was issued denying effectiveness to the statement and asking the respondent to appear before the Commission for examination. The Commission was thereupon advised of the registrant's intention to withdraw the statement. The right to withdraw was denied, however. The issue was carried to the Supreme Court of the United States, which assured registrants the unqualified right of withdrawal of registration statements prior to their having become effective. The Court, besides, reprimanded the Commission for its departure from the American tradition of security "against compulsory self accusation . . . unlawful searches and seizures . . . and unlawful inquisitorial investigations.''[80]

In the judgment of the Commission the problem is altogether different if a statement has become effective. The Oklahoma-Texas-Trust[81] sought the right to withdraw, sup-

---

[78]Rule 960, ''Any registration statement or any amendment thereto may be withdrawn upon the application of the registrant if the Commission, finding such withdrawal consistent with the public interest and the protection of investors, consents thereto. The application for such consent shall be signed by the registrant and shall state fully the grounds upon which made. The fee paid upon the filing of the registration statement will not be returned to the registrant. The papers comprising the registration statement or amendment thereto shall not be removed from the files of the Commission but shall be plainly marked with the date of the giving of such consent, and in the following manner: 'Withdrawn upon the request of the registrant, the Commission consenting thereto.' ''

[79]*Jones vs. Securities and Exange Commission.* 298 U. S. 1 (1936).

[80]*Ibid.* Dissenting, Mr. Justice Cardozo said: ''To permit an offending registrant to stifle an inquiry by precipitate retreat on the eve of his exposure is to give immunity to guilt; to encourage falsehood and evasion; to invite the cunning and unscrupulous to gamble with detection.''

[81]II Decisions 764.

porting its application with the argument that all the securities provided for in the statement had been distributed. The request was denied, however, because the securities were outstanding and "the rights of future potential investors to adequate and accurate information have come into being."[82] The opinion of the Commission in this case has been sustained in the United States Circuit Court of Appeals,[83] which said, in part, that "when the issuer files its registration statement, sells its securities, and places them in the channels of trade and commerce where they are likely to be sold . . . to third persons, the registration statement must remain on file for the benefit of such third persons."

A wholly different situation was presented by the case of Resources Corporation International. The day after this company's registration statement became effective, the Commission notified the registrant that its statement appeared to be deficient and that a hearing would occur at Washington. No securities had been sold and it was agreed that none would be sold pending determination of whether a stop order should be issued. The registrant made an effort to withdraw its statement but the Commission refused assent and the case was taken into court. Early in 1939 the United States Circuit Court of Appeals for the District of Columbia sustained the Commission.[84] The distinction between this case and the Jones case was "that the present registration had gone into effect" and that, in the judgment of the Court, was a "vital distinction." "If our view of the purpose of the legislation is correct," said the Court, "it will be seen at a glance how ineffective the pen-

---

[82]*Ibid.*, p. 772.
[83]100 Fed. (2nd) 888, 892 (1939).
[84]103 Fed. (2nd) 929 (1939). See also 97 Fed. (2nd) 788 (1938) and 24 Fed. Supp. 580 (1938).

alty provision would become if it be conceded that the registrant who has got the benefit of registration may, when charged with fraud in its procurement, withdraw and put an end to the inquisitorial powers of the Commission and escape the consequences of his wrong on the ground that no investor has suffered.'' If the opinion in this case revised the law, the Commission suffered no significant loss of power when the Supreme Court ruled against it in the Jones case.[85]

Stop Orders

''Where the examination and analysis of the registration statement disclose deficiencies but nevertheless reveal an honest attempt to meet the specified requirements, the registrant is advised of the deficiencies. In such case the deficiencies may be corrected by the filing of amendments. However, where the examination shows that the registration statement includes untrue statements or omissions of material facts which reflect intentional or reckless disregard of the standard of fair disclosure prescribed by the Act, stop order proceedings usually are instituted immediately.''[86]

It is the policy of the Commission, in each such instance, to have initial hearings held before a member of its staff who is designated as a trial examiner. The investigation may cover many months and involve elaborate testimony.[87] As soon as the hearing ends, the trial examiner must file with the Secretary of the Commission[88] a transcript of the

[85]*In the Matter of Marquette Mines, Inc.* S.E.C., Securities Act Release No. 2394, November 14, 1940. Withdrawal was allowed only on certain conditions specified by the Commission.

[86]*S.E.C., Fourth Annual Report*, p. 35.

[87]In the *National Boston Montana Mines Corporation Case* (I Decisions 639) the transcript of testimony covered more than 4500 pages. More than 600 exhibits were presented.

[88]In certain cases the report must be filed with the Commission. Rule IX(a).

record and "within 10 days after service upon him by the Secretary or other duly designated officer of the Commission of a copy of the transcript of the testimony" he is required to file a "report containing his findings of fact."[89] Within five days of the "receipt of a copy of the trial examiner's report, any party or counsel to the Commission may file exceptions to the findings of the trial examiner or to his failure to make findings, or to the admission or exclusion of evidence."[90] If any party, including counsel for the Commission, makes written request for it, the case will be heard by the entire Commission, provided the petition is filed within fifteen days of the trial examiner's report.[91] Notwithstanding the fact that the trial examiner is a member of the Commission's staff, his finding of fact is merely advisory.   In the Mutual Industrial Bankers, Inc.,[92] for example, the trial examiner filed a report which sustained the position of the registrant. Counsel for the Commission objected to this finding of fact and the Commission rejected the examiner's report.[93] After the Commission completes its hearing, at which the registrant is given opportunity to support its contentions, it either finds for the registrant or refuses to allow it to proceed with the sale of its securities.[94]

If a stop order is issued, the Commission may merely publish a brief statement of its findings or it may release a statement of the facts and of the reasons by which it was guided in reaching its decision. The latter procedure appears to be inspired by one or both of two different reasons: to condemn the registrant, and to warn and instruct in-

---

[89] Rule IX of Rules of Practice.   [91] Rule XII.
[90] Rule X.   [92] I Decisions 268.
[93] See also, *e.g.*, *Queensboro Gold Mines, Ltd.* II Decisions 860.
[94] For an illustration of a finding for the registrant, see II Decisions 675.

vestors and future issuers.[95] A registrant must inevitably lose prestige, if it possesses any, when the Commission publishes a formal opinion in connection with the issuance of a stop order against it and gives wide circulation to the opinion both by sending it to newspapers, financial agencies, and other organizations and citizens whose names are on its mailing list and by including it in bound volumes of its decisions which are kept in numerous libraries throughout the country. The fear of such adverse publicity is undoubtedly a restraining influence upon corporations preparing to sell new issues of securities.

But the Commission finds it possible through these opinions to acquaint issuers with the standards of truthfulness and the technique of reporting which it requires. Moreover, a published opinion may provide investors with warnings against devices designed to damage the unwary. It has, for example, warned against the "doodle bug" method of valuation;[96] it has publicized a registrant's "disregard of fundamental business ethics" and "unconscionable pretense of scientific method by an appraisal company;"[97] it has explained the implications of certain statements which untutored investors would not otherwise be likely to understand.[98]

The T. I. S. Management Corporation[99] pleaded with the Commission not to issue a stop order against it. It argued that the omissions were not important, that it had not in-

---

[95]"The purpose of a stop order," said the Commission in the Marquette Mines case (*op. cit.*), "is not solely to prevent the sale of securities . . . but is also to apprise . . . security holders of the actual facts and the falsity of statements included in the registration statement."

[96]*La Luz Mining Corporation.* I Decisions 217.

[97]I Decisions 47.

[98]*Gold Producers, Inc.,* I Decisions 1; *Lewis American Airways, Inc.,* I Decisions 330.

[99]III Decisions 174.

tended to mislead or defraud, that it was not only sympathetic with the purposes of the act, but had attempted to cooperate with the Commission in making corrections in its statement, that it would promise to provide its stockholders with copies of the amendments to its statement, that a stop order would be very damaging to its reputation, and that such action was unnecessary for the protection of investors or the public. But the Commission believed that the company's practices of trading "in trust shares to the detriment of the trust which it manages and at the cost of its shareholders precludes the exercise of our discretion in favor of the registrant in such a manner as to diminish that full notice of material deficiencies which is given by the issuance of stop orders."[100]

The power of the Commission to conduct investigations rests, fundamentally, upon the Securities Act itself which authorizes it to "subpena witnesses, take evidence, and require the production of any books, papers, or other documents which the Commission deems relevant or material to the inquiry."[101] Similar authority was given to the Federal Trade Commission at the time of its organization,[102] but Mr. Justice Holmes, speaking for the majority of the Supreme Court, declared that it would be difficult to "believe that Congress intended to authorize one of its subordinate agencies to sweep all our traditions into the fire and to direct fishing expeditions into private papers on the possibility that they may disclose evidence of crime."[103] It was to be expected that some registrant would seek umbrage, when threatened with an investigation, by pleading that a

---

[100]*Ibid.*, p. 183.
[101]Section 19(b).
[102]Section 9 of the Federal Trade Commission Act.
[103]*Federal Trade Commission vs. American Tobacco Company et al.* 264 U. S. 298 (1924).

proposed inquiry could be regarded as nothing more than a fishing expedition; and that is what happened when the Commission ordered Consolidated Mines of California to produce certain records. The Company had never registered its securities, but the Commission believed that it had been selling them in interstate commerce and through the use of the mails on the basis of false and misleading information. It had specific evidence to support this belief, but the company claimed constitutional immunity from being required to testify on the basis of the Supreme Court's pronouncement against "fishing expeditions." With this argument the court, which was asked to adjudicate the issue, was not impressed. It believed that the Commission had enough preliminary data to justify an inquiry and it ordered the respondent to produce its records.[104] Although the Supreme Court has not spoken upon this case, the law, so far as the judgment of this Circuit Court of Appeals is determinative, guarantees the Commission the right to require testimony and the production of records if it has enough preliminary evidence to provide support for a suspicion that the Act is being violated.

Meanwhile the power of Congress to regulate sales of securities in interstate commerce has been unsuccessfully challenged by the Oklahoma-Texas Trust.[105] The Court, sustaining the constitutionality of the Securities Act, declared that securities are subjects of commerce; that Congress did not forbid the sale of securities in intrastate commerce but required as a condition for distributing them in interstate commerce or through the mails, that certain facts be truthfully told; that the power of Congress to prevent

---

[104]*Consolidated Mines of California et al. vs. Securities and Exchange Commission,* 97 Fed. (2nd) 704 (1938).

[105]*Oklahoma-Texas Trust vs. Securities and Exchange Commission.* U. S. Circuit Court of Appeals (Tenth District), 100 Fed. (2nd) 888 (1939).

the use of the mails and the facilities of interstate commerce for the purpose of perpetrating fraud or as instruments of imposition has been well established in numerous judicial opinions.

Fraud

The Securities Act makes it illegal for any person "to employ any device, scheme, or artifice to defraud" or to get money or other property on the basis of an untrue or incomplete statement, or to defraud or deceive, or to give publicity to a security without disclosing any past or prospective compensation for such publicity. These prohibitions apply to transactions in all securities regardless of whether they are exempted from the requirement of registration.[106]

In 1935 the Commission established a "central index and clearing house for information relating to securities frauds in the United States and Canada, both past and current."[107] It cooperates with the Post Office Department, state blue sky commissions, public officials, and private organizations for the purpose of gathering information upon the activities of fraudulent dealers and bringing them to justice. The Commission is empowered to ask Federal courts for injunctions designed to put an end to the fraudulent activities of particular persons or it may make available to the Attorney General such information as it has that might seem to justify the institution of criminal proceedings. The Attorney General is under no obligation, however, to begin such action.[108]

---

[106]Securities Act, Section 17.

[107]*S.E.C., First Annual Report*, p. 35.

[108]Early in 1939 the Department of Justice established a Commercial Frauds Unit for the purpose of handling cases involving fraud including those which violate the Securities Act. See Release of Department of Justice, February 6, 1939.

CHAPTER VI

SIGNIFICANT FORMS OF MISREPRESENTATION

The most significant varieties of misrepresentation relate to the legal status of the registrant, the nature of the business, the relationships of issuers with promoters, the quality of management, and the valuation of property.

LEGAL STATUS OF THE REGISTRANT

The legal position of a registrant may easily be of great significance to investors. This is strikingly illustrated in the case of the Oklahoma-Texas Trust,[1] which reported in its registration statement that it was not a partnership. To this the Commission objected, notwithstanding the fact that the company had been organized as a business trust in conformity with Oklahoma statutes which granted to holders of the securities of such enterprises freedom from the personal liability to which general partners are subject.[2] The objection of the Commission was well sustained, for much of the property of the registrant was located in the State of Texas, which refuses to recognize the express trust. Instead, it regards the beneficiaries of all such organizations as partners and requires them to assume unlimited liability. The registrant sought to overcome this objection by claim-

---

[1] II Decisions 764.

[2] "Liability to third persons for any act, omission, or obligation of a trustee or trustees of an express trust, when acting in such capacity, shall extend to the whole of the trust estate held by such trustee or trustees, or so much thereof as may be necessary to discharge such liability but no personal liability shall attach to the trustees or the beneficiaries of such trust for any such act, omission or obligation." Chapter 62, Article 5 of Oklahoma Statutes (1931).

ing that its security holders were protected by the use of contracts requiring creditors to look only to the assets of the trust for the settlement of their claims against it. "While these measures undoubtedly reduce the risk of loss," the Commission replied, "they are only safeguards and cannot alter the basic fact if the participants are ultimately liable. Some forms of liability, such as the obligation to employees that they shall be recompensed for injuries received during the course of employment cannot be limited by contract on the ground that such a contract would be contrary to public policy."[3]

NATURE OF BUSINESS

The law requires each registrant to give a statement about the nature of its business. Usually "the answer to this item of registration is satisfied by a very brief description of the character of business done."[4] There are circumstances, however, under which simple answers are insufficient, for registrants may easily obscure the real nature of their business by neglecting to provide adequate information with respect to their past activities and achievements and with respect to their plans for the future.

Failure to Tell the Whole Truth about Past Activities

The Virginia City Gold Mining Company[5] alleged in its registration statement that its business had consisted exclusively of developing its properties. The mine which it had "developed" had, however, never been successful. The inability of the organization to earn profits in the past was

---

[3] II Decisions 777.
[4] I Decisions 343.
[5] II Decisions 855.

not made evident in the registration statement. Without knowledge of this past experience it did not seem to the Commission that prospective investors could have a clear understanding of what the registrant had been doing.

The Commonwealth Bond Corporation[6] reported that its principal business was "real estate bonds." Subsequent to 1930, however, it had actually sold no bonds but had devoted itself to "managing and insuring the property involved through its subsidiaries"[7] and to the reorganization of enterprises whose bonds it had sold when these enterprises found that they could no longer meet their obligations. That the registrant may have been a bond selling organization in the rather recent past[8] and that it probably hoped for a speedy revival of interest in real estate bonds which would enable it to abandon its work of reorganization were of no positive significance to the Commission. The business "now being done by the respondent"[9] had to be described in order to give satisfactory information.

The American Gyro Company[10] declared that its principal business would be "to develop and perfect mechanical devices."[11] It said nothing about the fact that it was engaged in the printing business nor that some of its capital had been used for purposes other than those mentioned. It had committed a portion of its capital to the "support of enterprises not disclosed in the registration statement"[12] and some of its resources had been used for the private advantage of one of its own promoters. These facts were enough to persuade the Commission that the registrant had not told the truth.

---

[6] I Decisions 19.
[7] *Ibid.*
[8] The opinion of the Commission was promulgated on May 23, 1934.
[9] I Decisions 19. [11] *Ibid.*, p. 85.
[10] *Ibid.*, 83. [12] *Ibid.*

The Emporia Gold Mines, Inc.,[13] asserted in its registration statement that its principal business had been the preparation of "the mining property to resume operations of actually working the mine." That the property needed preparation at the time the statement became effective is evidenced by the fact that the mine was full of water to "within 50 or 60 feet of the surface"[14] and that both of its shafts were caved, one of them being "filled with rock and timber in a crater-like hole."[15] It was the judgment of the Commission that the registrant had not told the truth in its statement of the nature of its business. Although it had not produced as much as ten tons of ore prior to the inquiry of the Commission,[16] it had sold over thirty-five thousand shares of its one dollar par value stock. The net return for the ore had been $59.83. The net proceeds from the sale of stock had been $25,337.70. On May 1, 1936, it had in its treasury the sum of $3.53. It had, however, paid a salary in excess of six thousand dollars to each of two men who were instrumental in its promotion and who subsequently became its principal officers. In addition the promoters had received 250,000 shares of stock. The Commission decided, with apparent propriety, that Emporia Gold Mines, Inc., was not so much a mining venture as a stock selling scheme.[17]

---

[13]II Decisions 209.
[14]II Decisions 213.
[15]*Ibid.*
[16]The company was organized June 1, 1933. Its registration statement was effective January 15, 1935. Hearings were held by the Commission in November and December, 1936. A stop order was issued April 23, 1937.
[17]Similar in this respect is the case (II Decisions 551) of *Canusa Gold Mines, Limited.* Although the company declared that it had conducted "the business of exploration, development, mining, reduction, and refining of gold and other mineral bearing ores," the Commission became convinced that "its major activities since its creation in 1932 have been confined to the sale of its capital stock."

Failure to Tell the Truth about Future Plans

The difficulty of eliciting reliable information about what a corporation expects to do with money to be obtained from the sale of securities presently to be issued is illustrated by the experience which the Commission had with the Corporate Leaders Securities Company.[18] Early in 1936 this company filed a registration statement, which, after it had been amended four times, in due course became effective. Those about to buy its securities were informed that the company intended "to subscribe for, purchase, hold, sell, underwrite or otherwise deal in all forms of securities generally. The officers and directors of this company are all officers and/or directors of Corporate Leaders of America, Inc. . . . and it is intended to participate in the distribution of the securities of that company. The terms and conditions of such intention or the entire scope thereof are not now known, but will be determined from time to time when and as business is done."[19] In its prospectus it advertised that it expected to own the "obligations and securities of mercantile, industrial, and financial corporations."

Such objectives as these were in harmony with existing public policy and there was no reason for questioning the sincerity of those who established them for this particular company. The accuracy of all such statements of intent can be tested only after those who make them have had an opportunity to demonstrate the quality of their trusteeship of other people's money. The Commission might never have been inspired to apply the test in this case had it not been for the fact that, in order to continue the distribution of its securities under the registration statement of 1936, the Corporate Leaders Securities Company was required

[18] II Decisions 667.
[19] Registrant's answer to Item 3, Registration Statement File 2-1865.

early in April, 1937, to furnish the Commission with a thirteen months prospectus.[20]   The filing of this document started an inquiry which resulted in the discovery that as of the date of the thirteen months prospectus, the registrant had an investment of approximately fifty thousand dollars in the securities of the Corporate Leaders of America, Inc.; that it owned all of the preferred and eighty per cent of the common stock of the latter corporation; and that it had not invested in any other company one cent of the money which it obtained from the sale of the securities originally registered in 1936.

Without manifesting the slightest interest as to whether the investment of funds in the affiliate had been advantageous to the security holders of the registrant the Commission concluded that the nature of its business had not been correctly stated when it reported its intention of investing "in all forms of securities generally."   On the basis of this finding, and this alone, the Commission issued a stop order.

If an issuer expects to sell only a portion of the securities which it registers, that fact must be indicated in the registration statement.   The United Combustion Corporation[21] declared that it intended to offer one thousand shares of common and five hundred shares of preferred at the total par value of $51,000.   The president of the company testified before a trial examiner, however, that $51,000 was an "outside figure"; that the company had two plans in mind, one of which would require about ten thousand dollars, the other three times as much; that it expected to sell new stock

---

[20] "When a prospectus is used more than thirteen months after the effective date of the registration statement, the information in the statements contained therein shall be as of a date not more than twelve months prior to such use, so far as such information is known to the user of such prospectus or can be furnished by such user without unreasonable effort or expense." Securities Act, Section 10 (b) (1).

[21] III Decisions 1062.

only to the extent necessary for obtaining the required capital. It was the opinion of the Commission that the "investor is entitled to know the amount of capital which the registrant is presently seeking. Moreover, it would be contrary to the obvious intent of the Securities Act to permit the registration of more securities than are presently intended to be offered, and thus give securities offered at some remote future time at least the appearance of a registered status."[22]

The name of a business organization may give an erroneous impression of the activities in which it engages. The Commission was of the opinion that the National Educators Mutual Association, Inc., deliberately sought to have the public associate it with the National Education Association.[23] The promoter of the company admitted in testimony before the Commission that the name of the company could be misleading. There was objection, too, to the word *Mutual,* for the company was organized for the exclusive benefit of those who were identified with it as officers and stockholders.[24]

The Major Metals Corporation[25] had been "engaged in gathering data concerning commercial ore mining properties in the United States which had blocked out ore and

---

[22]*Ibid.,* 1063.

[23]I Decisions 213.

[24]This company would have sold, had the Commission allowed its statement to become effective, units consisting in each case of a "5-annual payment, 10 year endowment bond, with 5 shares of stock." It was expected the purchaser of each unit would agree to pay $150.00 a year for five years. At the end of ten years the company would pay the holder $750 in cash and five shares of stock with a stated value of $50.00 a share. The bond, however, promised to pay the owner one thousand dollars. This statement appeared prominently on the bond, followed by another statement in parenthesis and in small type, "consisting of $750 cash and $250 stock." The Commission found this usage "untrue and misleading."

[25]II Decisions 76.

were for sale.''[26]   It planned to make an examination of these and other properties with the objective of purchasing and operating some of them.   In order to accomplish this purpose the company proposed the issue of $5,000,000, par value, ten-year, six per cent debenture bonds.   The company later decided to drop the word *bonds,* because the obligations represented unsecured claims.   There was, besides, no ''provision in the terms of the debentures for the acceleration of any claims for future interest or for the principal sum due in 1947.''[27]   After the hearings began, the registrant became convinced that there was considerable uncertainty as to whether it could pay interest during the first two years of the life of the debentures and it therefore indicated willingness to offer them subject to the condition that no interest would be paid during that period.   This did not satisfy the Commission, however.   An expert in mining engineering told the Commission that to examine a single mine in the way the company said it intended to do would require the services of a mining engineer and a group of assistants for a period of from one to three months.   It has often been impossible, besides, for companies which have had experience with new properties to bring them into operation for a period of two years or more after acquiring them.   Even when it is possible to bring them into profitable operation within a shorter period, it is ordinarily impractical to make immediate payment of interest and dividends out of income obtained from new property.   ''This situation arises from the fact that experience within the industry has shown it to be necessary to plow back into the business all initially reported operating income to insure adequate development

---

[26]The list of properties about which preliminary information had already been compiled consisted of five hundred units.

[27]II Decisions 77.

work and final success of operation.''[28] The company in an amendment called the attention of possible purchasers of its debentures to the fact that new developments sometimes become profitable only after three or four years of exploitation; but it expected to choose its properties so wisely that it would most certainly be able to pay interest within a period of two years. With this change the Commission was not impressed. In its judgment the history of the mining industry offered very little evidence to support the claims of the registrant. ''While it is not within the province of the Commission to pass upon the merits of the many plans for financing which pass before it, it is within the scope of its duties to insist that all plans, whether of a highly speculative nature or otherwise, shall be described in language which in no way veils the essential character of the particular plan under consideration.''[29]

THE RELATIONSHIPS OF ISSUERS WITH PROMOTERS

There has often been extraordinary secrecy in the relationships of issuers with promoters. This is to be explained on the ground that promoters have frequently desired large profits for themselves from the sale of property and substantial rewards for their promotional activities. The fruition of such hopes is most likely when their business arrangements with issuers are grounded in secrecy. With two varieties of such secrecy the Commission has had to contend: attempts to hide information as to who the promoters are, and attempts to hide information as to the magnitude of the promoters' rewards.

---

[28]*Ibid.*, p. 76.
[29]*Ibid.*, p 77.

Attempts to Hide Information about Promoters

The courts have never defined the word *promoter* as it is used in the Securities Act. Nor has the Commission been able or willing to do so with precision. Morawetz says that the "word 'promoter' has no technical meaning, and applies to any person who takes an active part in inducing the formation of a company, whether he afterwards becomes connected with the company or not."[30] Apparently accepting this statement, which it quotes, the Commission observes that a promoter has generally been regarded as a "person who enters into a common enterprise with other persons to form a corporation, transfer property to it, and sell stock to the public." It is "broad enough to include one who, in concert with the actual incorporators, purchases property with the intent to sell it to an enterprise yet to be formed and to receive his compensation from the purchase price of securities to be distributed to the public. How much broader the term is we need not decide."[31]

Although it is probably not difficult to identify promoters in most instances, there are border line cases in which it is far from easy to say whether any particular persons are to be classified as promoters or not. This is exemplified in the matter of the Oklahoma-Texas Trust.[32] Counsel for the Commission believed that the son-in-law of one of the promoters of this organization should have been included among the promoters. Although he had no share in the organization of the trust or in the distribution of its securities, he did take part in a conference with the trustees for consideration of the purchase, through his father-in-law, of

---

[30]Morawetz, *Private Corporations*, p. 545.
[31]*Oklahoma-Texas Trust*, II Decisions 774, 775.
[32]*Ibid.*, 775.

additional property of substantial value,[33] and received without consideration an assignment of a claim to a portion of the promoters' profits. These facts did not persuade the Commission, however, that he was a promoter.

Failure to reveal the identity of promoters is not uncommon. The National Boston Montana Mines Corporation had arisen as a result of a series of reorganizations of corporations that had without exception been unprofitable to their owners.[34] The registration statement declared that the principal promoter of the registrant was a man who had been dominant in the affairs of all its predecessors. The Commission decided, however, that the names of four other persons should have been included in the list of promoters. To one of these four the company had agreed to issue six million shares in exchange for an interest which he had in some property in Mexico. The registration statement did not disclose, however, the existence of a secret agreement for the distribution of a portion of these shares among the other three. ''All of them jointly were instrumental in organizing the registrant, which, while it took over the assets of a predecessor, was in final analysis a new corporation formed to develop a mining property which had never been successfully operated, which was still in the developmental stage, and which was to be financed by public subscription.''[35]

The complexity of the problem of untangling the relationships of promoters with registrants is illustrated in the case of the Equity Corporation.[36] For the sake of simplicity in exposition a letter will be assigned to each company except

---

[33]This conference occurred two or three months after the registration statement became effective.
[34]II Decisions 226.
[35]II Decisions 244.
[36]II Decisions 675.

the Equity.[37] One of its promoters owned all the stock of A, which in turn owned 1,150,000 shares of the stock of the Equity. These shares had been obtained by *A* in exchange for some three hundred thousand shares in *B*. As a consequence of this transaction Equity was now able to control *C*. Two of the directors of Equity had indirect control over *D*, which had a controlling interest in *E*. Stock in *F* and *G* constituted practically all the assets of *E*. Approximately $900,000 worth of stock in *F* and *G* were sold by *E* to *C* for cash; $700,000 of this sum was then used by *E* for the purchase of stock in *H*, which immediately bought of *A* one million of its shares in the Equity Corporation for $700,000 in cash and a note for $200,000. In this devious manner the promoter, in the judgment of the Commission, made a profit "well in excess of $500,000."[38]

Attempts to Hide Information as to Promoters' Pay

The principal problem of the Commission in dealing with the matter of promoters' pay has evidently been to get frank statements from issuers regarding promoters' compensation. A very common method of obscuring the amount of a promoter's reward is to issue an excessive amount of stock under circumstances which ultimately leave a portion of it in the promoter's possession. The Unity Gold Corporation provides an excellent example.[39] For five thousand dollars in cash and 599,995 shares of its one dollar par value stock it obtained certain property. The seller was

---

[37] *A*, Compania Montana, a Panama corporation; *B*, Yosemite Holding Corporation; *C*, Interstate Equities Corporation; *D*, Consolidated Funds of New York; *E*, Underwriters Equities, Inc.; *F*, American Colony Insurance Company; *G*, Colonial States Fire Insurance Company; *H*, Oceanic Life Insurance Company, Ltd.

[38] *Ibid.*, 686.

[39] I Decisions 25.

required to return 475,000 shares as a donation to the issuer, and the principal promoter of the corporation and his associates were given all the 124,995 remaining shares. The registrant reported to the Commission that its property had cost $604,995. The balance sheet gave no indication that promoters had ever received anything for their services. Although the Commission found no fault with the practice of rewarding promoters, it did not believe that promoters' fees could "be deemed to be so intimately connected with the purchase of the property as to justify their inclusion in the cost of the latter without, at least, segregating them. . . . Accounting theory and practice reveal some disagreement as to whether such expenses are properly to be regarded as representing capital assets or should be treated as a deferred or prepaid expense, but there is no disagreement that expenses in the nature of promoters' fees should be listed separately from expenditures representing the consideration paid for physical property.'"[40]

In a few instances the Commission has concerned itself with the magnitude of promoters' rewards. The balance sheet which the Brandy-Wine Brewing Company filed very frankly stated that the promoter had been rewarded by an issue of $71,000 of stock.[41] The board of directors had formally valued the services of the promoter and had declared its conviction that they were worth $71,000. The laws of many states—among them Delaware, the state in which this corporation was organized—make the judgments of boards of directors in all such matters conclusive in the absence of fraud. The Securities and Exchange Commission refuses, however, to be bound by such a policy. A license to sell securities in interstate commerce requires

---

[40]*Ibid.*, p. 30.
[41]I Decisions 123.

compliance with federal law, even though there is no specific provision in the Securities Act giving the Commission power to set aside the judgment of a board of directors in valuing property or services. Proper application of the doctrine of truthfulness makes it mandatory for the Commission to satisfy itself that boards of directors manifest good faith and hence a spirit of integrity in arriving at valuations. If it finds that any board has not dealt with the problem of valuation in such a spirit, it is then appropriate for the Commission to declare the registration statement deficient and to require modification as a condition for the future distribution of its securities.

Although the Commission was unwilling to be bound in the Brandy-Wine Brewing Company case by that provision of Delaware law relating to the finality of valuations by boards of directors, it found another law of that state which forbade the issuance of stock for services to be rendered in the future. The stock which the promoter was to receive could not be in excess of the value of services rendered in the past. An examination of the history of these services revealed that they had been negligible in importance; that they had been "so grossly and indefensibly excessive as to be outside the range of reasonable difference of opinion."[42]

The Commission has expressed concern over promoters' claims to corporate income if these claims are excessive when compared to their investments. It called public attention to the fact that the investment of the principal promoter of the Lewis American Airways, Inc.,[43] was to be only two per cent of the total contributed capital but that his ownership of stock would be such as to make it possible for him to get fifty-one per cent of corporate earnings. Had

---

[42]*Ibid.*, p. 136.
[43]I Decisions 330.

the Commission not interfered by issuing a stop order, the public would have been asked to contribute over ninety per cent of the capital and allow control to be vested in the promoter. In its published opinion the Commission felt it worth while to remark upon the fact that the charter forbade cumulative voting and hence that public stockholders could not be influential in managing the corporation.

QUALITY OF MANAGEMENT

Although the quality of management of a corporation is of preeminent importance to those who already own or are about to buy its securities, there are obvious difficulties in trying to get data with which to evaluate it. Inferences as to the quality of management may be drawn from information upon such matters as the character of experience of those in managerial positions, the character of their actual or prospective relationships with security holders, the character of the contracts to which they are parties or to which they have committed or propose to commit the issuer, and the character of the claims which management makes for the registrant.

Character of Experience of Those in Managerial Positions

The American Credit Corporation[44] stated in its prospectus that its president had for eighteen years been engaged in the automobile finance and insurance brokerage business; that companies with which he had been identified in managerial capacities during that period had handled approximately fifteen million dollars' worth of obligations arising from installment sales of automobiles. The Commission found that, although the president of the company

---

[44] I Decisions 230.

had been associated with a great many organizations, "one searches in vain . . . for one corporation which can present a picture of consistent and successful operation."[45] It discovered, besides, that the experience of this man had been such that neither the registrant nor any other corporation under his control would be permitted to sell securities in California, the state under whose laws the registrant had been organized.

The principal promoter and officer of the Sunbeam Gold Mines Company[46] had been dominant in the affairs of numerous enterprises, all of which he had managed according to the same pattern. His plan was to sell mining property to a corporation at about the time its campaign for selling stock got under way. As funds were accumulated in consequence of the sale of stock, they were used for expenses, including payment of the salary of the principal promoter and officer. As funds were exhausted, stockholders were asked to make loans to the corporation, "the usual motif being the statement that with but a few extra dollars the metaphorical gold mine could be developed into a bonanza." Thereafter stockholders were asked to subscribe to new shares at reduced prices.

The prospectus issued by the Gilpin Eureka Consolidated Mines, Inc., in 1934[47] declared that its president had had four years' experience as an engineer for the Austrian government and that for the last three years he had been engaged in the business of mining engineering. Two years after the statement of this registrant became effective the Commission initiated an inquiry and discovered that the president's experience with the Austrian government had

---

[45]*Ibid.*, p. 234.
[46]III Decisions 299.
[47]I Decisions 752.

"consisted of driving and overhauling locomotives of the government-owned railroad" and that "his training in mining consisted of reading of textbooks and conversation with mining people."[48]

Character of the Relationships Between the Management and Security Holders

The character of the relationships between management and security holders is often exemplified by the types of contracts which those in official positions make or propose to make with security holders and by the methods that management uses in handling problems which affect the financial well being of security holders.

In the summer of 1939 Free Traders, Inc., proposed the issuance of priority common stock. The ordinary common stockholders were to have exclusive voting power unless the corporation failed to pay dividends to the priority common stockholders during any two successive fiscal years. In case of such failure the two classes of stockholders were to have equal voting power. The ordinary stockholders were to be entitled to ten per cent of all net earnings actually distributed. The priority common stockholders were not to have any prior claim to earnings, however, and the management was to have the privilege of allocating to earned surplus as much as sixty-five per cent of net earnings whenever it seemed desirable to do so. In the event of liquidation the priority common could claim ninety per cent of the capital, capital surplus, and earned surplus. Any priority common shareholder was, moreover, to have the right under certain conditions to surrender his stock and receive in

---

[48]I Decisions 757. For further illustrations, see *Reiter-Foster Case*, VI Decisions 1058; and *In the Matter of Petroleum Investors Participating Association*, S.E.C., Securities Act Release No. 2413, December 4, 1940.

exchange his share of the "net liquidated asset value " of the company.

The Commission found a great many reasons for objecting to this proposed contract. In the first place directors could "declare dividends out of surplus" and hence "it would appear to be possible for them to limit further the right of holders of priority common to vote by declaring nominal dividends even in the absence of current earnings." In the second place, only 10,200 shares of the ordinary common were outstanding and all of these had been issued to the promoters for "services."[49] It was proposed, however, to issue 200,000 shares of one dollar priority common. "Consequently," said the Commission, "if the 200,000 shares of priority common are issued, the holder of each share will receive as dividends less than one-half as much per share as the holders of ordinary common. Thus, on the assumption that the 200,000 shares of priority common are sold and that at the end of the first year $10,000 is distributed as a dividend, 90% or $9000 will be distributed to 200,000 shares of priority common, which is equal to 4½c per share, while 10% or $1000 will be distributed to the 10,200 shares of ordinary common, which will be almost 10c per share."

In the third place, the liquidation rights did not appear upon careful examination to be very attractive. The ordiary common shares had a book value of twenty-five cents or an aggregate stated value of $2,550. Assuming the sale of two hundred thousand shares of priority common at a dollar a share, there could hardly be "substance in the argument that the term 'priority' is justified merely be-

---

[49] Of these services the Commission said: "There is no clear indication in the record of the kind of services rendered by the promoters as consideration for this stock."

cause the charter provides that the stock will be entitled on liquidation to what is left of the asset of $2,550, in addition to capital and capital surplus contributed by priority common stockholders.''

Finally, the right of redemption would, under certain circumstances, be without value. This right could not be exercised at all should the net asset value happen to be less than a dollar a share for the priority common. In any case there was to be a ''service charge of 5c a share with a minimum of $1 for each redemption transaction. If the value of the priority common declines appreciably, the service charge becomes an important factor, particularly in the case of those investors who hold small blocks.''[50]

The character of the relationships between management and security holders is further exemplified by the methods that are employed in handling problems which are vital to the financial welfare of security holders. Significant among such problems are the computation of corporate income, the development of devices which are employed for rewarding those in managerial positions, and the payment of dividends.

The management of the Illinois Zinc Company concealed from its auditors and the public a substantial shortage in zinc concentrate inventories caused by excessive dust losses.''[51] Late in 1937 the shortage reached ''approximately 1200 tons of concentrates, valued at $35,767.41.'' One of the officials of the company thought that the shortage should be ''charged to the current year's operations or to surplus, or both, depending upon the facts, and that the matter be reported to the board of directors.''[52] To this

---

[50]All the quotations are from VII Decisions 913. See also the case of the Chain Stores Depot Corporation, VII Decisions 1015.
[51]VI Decisions 852.
[52]*Ibid.*, p. 853.

the president would not agree. The shortage was eliminated by keeping no record of production at two of the company's mills throughout the month of November, 1937, and capitalizing "the actual cost of production for the month as development."[53] The Commission concluded that the reported profits had been overstated by several thousand dollars.

The W. Wallace Alexander Fund, Inc.,[54] had sold units of participation in accordance with an agreement that ninety per cent of the income and profits available for distribution should be paid to owners of these units and the remainder should be paid to management. Although management had the right to determine the amount that could be distributed, the sum available for distribution in any year could not exceed current income and trading profits. Trading profits consisted of net profits obtained from the sale of securities which the Fund had obtained since June 30, 1932. Profits and losses upon securities purchased prior to that date were to be considered as additions to or deductions from capital. The opportunity which application of this formula gave the management to obtain more than ten per cent of the income is exemplified by its compensation for 1936. The Commission declared that for that year "the net income and profits of the Fund, computed in accordance with sound principles of accounting, amounted to $106,-789.29. On that basis the management's commission should not have exceeded $10,678.93. However, $21,598.06 was appropriated as commissions to the management during that year."

In the Matter of Resources Corporation International the Commission untangled the complicated relationships which

---

[53]*Ibid.*, p. 853.
[54]VI Decisions 127, 134.

existed between the registrant and its principal promoter.[55] The promoter had received a good deal of the registrant's stock but had "never spent one mill of his own funds in this venture." It was the practice of the company, which owned timber lands, to enter into timber-cutting contracts with other organizations. Contractors were required, in at least a good many instances, to make down payments in cash to the Resources Corporation International. Some of these contractors were without financial responsibility and the principal promoter of the registrant made personal loans to such contractors in order that they might fulfill their obligations to make down payments. The promoter "did not consider that the advances made by him were of any value as an aid to the commencement of operations for . . . he deemed his advances of such little value as investments that he either sold interests representing such advances at tremendous discounts or wrote off as losses substantially the entire amount of the sums advanced within a short time after such advances were made."[56] The man who made these advances was not only the principal promoter; he was dominant in the affairs of the corporation. He was able, therefore, "immediately upon the receipt of these moneys" by the corporation to bring about the distribution "of the great bulk thereof to shareholders . . . without regard to the desirability of retaining funds with which to assist timber-cutting contractors to commence operations or for any other corporate purposes."[57] It was the belief of the Commission that these arrangements "greatly facilitated the sale to the public" of the stock which the principal promoter had in his possession.

---

[55]*Resources Corporation, International.* VII Decisions 689.
[56]*Ibid.*, p. 713.
[57]*Ibid.*

Contracts Between a Registrant and Its Officers

The income of those who manage a corporation is of fundamental importance under the Securities Act. The Commission is interested in nothing more than an accurate record of the rewards that have been obtained for managerial services. The problem of getting the facts is exemplified in the case of the National Boston Montana Mines Corporation.[58] Its registration statement, as amended, declared that no director was then receiving compensation in any form nor had any director received compensation during the preceding year. The Commission discovered, however, that three of the directors had no other income save that which they received from the sale of registrant's stock; that all of them received payments "which were never accounted for as expenses, and it was understood that these payments were family allowances."[59]

Important, too, are records of sales of property by officers and directors to the corporations which they manage. Tampax, Inc., was obliged to amend its original statement, chiefly, it would seem, because it had failed to give a satisfactory account of a contract involving the purchase of certain intangible assets.[60] In its original statement patents, trade mark and goodwill were valued at $571,225.40 but there was nothing to indicate how this figure had been chosen. The amendment, however, stated frankly that of the eleven members of the board of directors four were promoters or representatives of promoters; that two of these were also representatives of the sellers of the patents and trade mark which Tampax had purchased; that the value

[58] II Decisions 226.
[59] *Ibid.*, p. 242.
[60] File Number 2-2498-1. B. B. Greidinger, *Accounting Requirements of the Securities and Exchange Commission*, p. 246. New York (1939).

of patents and trade marks had been fixed by the board; that this valuation had not been based on earnings; and that the cost to the vendor of the patents and trade marks sold to the registrant "and of certain French and German patents not transferred" had been $57,446.75. With these disclosures the statement was allowed to become effective.

The genuineness of a contract between a registrant and a group of well known persons who were advertised as members of its board of directors was examined by the Commission in the case of the National Invested Savings Corporation.[61] The pictures and biographies of the directors appeared in the prospectus followed by the names of the "General Committee of National Founders." This committee consisted of friends of the directors who as "founders" were to be privileged to buy stock on preferential terms in exchange for a promise to render certain services to the company in the future.[62] "The purpose of a display of this character is not difficult to penetrate," said the Commission. "It gives the impression to innocent investors that this group of well known and presumably successful persons is giving its time and effort to building a highly worthy enterprise and that some safety to the investors springs from that fact."[63] In a later opinion involving the same company[64] the Commission issued a retraction of that part of the accusation which related to the board of directors. The company had not been allowed to sell its securities but its business was nevertheless continued and many of those

[61] I Decisions 825. Among those named as directors were a former U. S. senator, two former members of Congress, a present member of Congress, a brigadier general in the army, a retired rear admiral.
[62] The Commission was of the opinion that "the legality of the issuance of common stock to the founders for consideration in the nature of services to be rendered in the future is, under Delaware law, seriously open to question." II Decisions 116.
[63] I Decisions 830.
[64] II Decisions 113.

persons whose pictures appeared in the prospectus participated actively in its management. The Commission admitted that its "earlier conclusion in this respect was in error."[65] In its former opinion the Commission stated that the general committee never met; that those who organized it had no intention that it should meet; that its members were expected to do nothing more than buy stock and sponsor the introduction to their acquaintances of persons acting as sales representatives for an insurance company which was a subsidiary of the registrant. The subsequent inquiry by the Commission adduced no evidence to justify a modification of its previous opinion that the prospectus did not tell the truth about this Committee.

Because an investment trust offers management a peculiar opportunity to use company resources for the interests of special groups, the Commission felt that the Investment Company of North America[66] should have given a clear indication of the relationships between the two men who controlled it. "The management of an investment trust with no more limitation on its selection of investments than is contained in the charter of the registrant, may direct the corporation's activities into any one of a countless number of businesses. The advantages which may be gained from obtaining control over such a source of credit are obvious. Equally obvious is the danger that investments may not always be made for the benefit of the corporation's security holders." As a matter of experience some of the assets of this registrant had been used in rendering assistance to certain other organizations with which the management was identified.

---

[65] *Ibid.*, p. 115.
[66] V Decisions 287, 291.

Contracts Between a Registrant and Affiliated Parties

The Commission evidently believes that every material contract between a registrant and each affiliate ought to be reported, however tenuous the relationships between the two may be.[67] The Consolidated Funds Corporation of Delaware was organized in 1933. In its original registration statement it announced its plan to buy all of the assets of the Consolidated Funds Corporation of New York except its franchise to be a corporation. The New York corporation had an indirect interest in the Oceanic Insurance Company, Ltd., which had an option to buy 150,000 shares of stock in the Equity Corporation.[68] The exercise of this option by the Oceanic Corporation would give control of the Equity to the New York corporation. The Commission was of the opinion that the terms of this contract should have been reported.[69]

Contracts Between a Registrant and Outsiders

It is difficult to see how the Commission could concern itself with the content of a contract between a registrant and persons having no direct or indirect relationship with it as promoters, officers, or principal stockholders, except to inquire into the genuineness and the completeness of the registrant's representations regarding it. The Brandy-Wine Brewing Company[70] having estimated that property

---

[67]Some registrants have been unwilling to publicize, voluntarily, those relationships which make them affiliates of other organizations. The Commission has defined a parent of a specified person as "an affiliate controlling such person directly, or indirectly through one or more intermediaries" and an affiliate as "a person that directly, or indirectly through one or more intermediaries, controls, or is controlled by, or is under common control with, the person specified." Rule 455.

[68]This stock in the Equity Corporation was owned by Compania Montana.

[69]For a discussion of other contracts not reported by this same registrant see II Decisions 728-729.

[70]I Decisions 123.

in which it was interested contained 1,200,000 yards of sand and gravel, entered into a written contract which required the purchaser to buy it at the rate of 120,000 yards a year. There were two aspects of this contract to which the Commission objected. It was of the opinion that the company had been overoptimistic in estimating the aggregate supply of gravel and sand, and it was convinced, after careful inquiry, that the buyer had not only been ignorant of the terms of the contract he signed, but could not possibly fulfill his commitments under it, both because of his limited financial resources and because of the certainty that a market for the amount of sand and gravel which he was expected to buy could not be found.

Character of the Claims Made by Management

Light is sometimes shed upon the quality of management by claims which a registrant makes for itself. The American Kid Company estimated that its annual earnings in the immediate future would approximate thirty-six per cent of its invested capital.[71] In attacking the truthfulnes of this claim the Commission relied upon the testimony of a specialist in leather, a member of the staff of the Department of Commerce, who said that he did not know of any manufacturer of kid leather with an earnings experience over the preceding five years much better than a third as good as the registrant anticipated for itself.

This same company claimed that the branch of the industry to which it belonged was not subject to the same severity of competition as that with which independent tanners were confronted. From this judgment, however, the Commission dissented; it pointed out that there were numerous im-

---

[71] I Decisions 694.

portant producers of kid leather in the United States and that the competition among them, already very keen, had but recently been accentuated because of a decline in the demand for kid leather. Changing fashions in shoes, moreover, had impaired the position of the existing producers of kid leather.

The American Terminals and Transit Company[72] was certain, according to its prospectus, that it had secured control of the retail coal market in Evansville, Indiana. The president of the company estimated that this market had an annual capacity of from seven hundred and fifty thousand to a million tons. The estimate of the local chamber of commerce was even higher. An expert testifying for the Commission was of the opinion, however, that three hundred and fifty thousand tons was a more reasonable estimate; of this amount the Commission believed the registrant could not possibly be asked to provide as much as forty-eight thousand tons. The company justified its use of the word *control* by claiming that because it was the low bidder on a public contract in the local market, it was able to fix the prices in that market. At about the same time, however, the Commission discovered that the company was underbid on another contract.

The Mining and Development Corporation[73] believed that it might expect profits in excess of a million dollars a year from mining property in Bolivia. Support for this opinion came largely from a 1928 report of a mining engineer. Subsequent to that date a great many things happened to modify the economic position of Bolivian mining interests of which the average American investor might have remained in ignorance had it not been for the publicity which

[72] I Decisions 701.
[73] I Decisions 786.

the Commission gave to them in its formal opinion in this case. In 1931, for example, Bolivia became a party to an international tin cartel. The tonnage assigned to Bolivia by this cartel was distributed by the Government among the various mines. The quota assigned to the registrant had amounted to but little more than four hundred tons per year. In the judgment of the Commission its profits could not equal the amount claimed in the registration statement and prospectus "with a production of less than 3600 tons per year of fine tin."[74]   In 1928, moreover, Bolivia was on the gold standard. At the time of the Commission's inquiry Bolivian foreign exchange was under such rigid control that not all of the profits that the company might make could become available for the payment of dividends upon the stock which it proposed to issue; "some 35% of its net profits from the Bolivian mines . . . would thus either not be available at all for payment of dividends . . . or else would suffer a minimal 50 per cent shrinkage in transmission, by virtue of this phase of the Bolivian system of exchange control."[75]

The prospectus of Thomas Bond, Inc.,[76] declared that its preparation would conquer "lines, blackheads, oily skins, and coarse pores." The Commission learned that this claim was unfounded, and officers of the registrant testified at the hearings that the preparation "merely concealed these conditions."

It has been easy for certain managements—particularly those interested in mining ventures—to underestimate future costs of production. This is illustrated in the U. S. Chromium case.[77]   The promoter and president of the com-

---

[74]*Ibid.*, 801.
[75]*Ibid.*, 803.
[76]V Decisions 60, 70.
[77]VI Decisions 882.

pany who, according to the trial examiner, was a "thoroughly unreliable and untrustworthy witness," expressed the belief that the company would be able to mine two thousand tons of ore daily through the use of the hydraulic method. He estimated that three tons of water would be sufficient for each ton of ore mined and that the cost of mining would amount to three cents a ton. A mining expert in the employ of the Commission was of the opinion, however, that the amount of water necessary for mining a ton of the registrant's ore was more than twice as great as the estimate of the president, and that three cents "a ton for hydraulicking was much too low and ran contrary to general experience."[78]

Judgments regarding the quality of management are likely to be colored by the registrant's failure to disclose any difficulties with which it is or is about to be confronted. The Petroleum Investors Participating Association stated in its proposed prospectus that if it could have "a reasonable degree of success, it is believed that a minimum of 6% per annum return on each participating certificate will be earned." The Commission concluded that inasmuch as the company had never done business, this claim could hardly have any validity; it felt, too, that "the failure to indicate anywhere in the prospectus the adverse factors which presently exist in the oil industry, as indicated by the record, and which will affect the value of the securities in which the registrant proposes to invest, makes the impression created by this statement all the more false."[79]

VALUATION OF PROPERTY

Getting issuers to tell the truth about the value of their property has been one of the most significant problems

---

[78]*Ibid.*, p. 897.
[79]S.E.C., Securities Act Release No. 2413, December 4 ,1940.

with which the Commission has had to deal. Not only have they been optimistic in their opinions as to the value of such intangible items as goodwill and patent rights; they have frequently placed excessive values on tangible property. In judging the validity of these valuations the Commission has been interested in costs and appraisals.

Cost of Property

The practice of issuing stock for property or services as fully paid, with the understanding that some of the shares should be returned to the corporation as a gift, has had a long history. The Unity Gold Corporation[80] resorted to this practice and sought to justify it before the Commission by calling attention to the fact that the state under whose laws it had been organized authorized directors to issue stock in exchange for property with the presumption, in the absence of positive evidence to the contrary, that it had been fully paid for even though some of the stock might be returned to the corporation simultaneously as a donation. The Commission refused to be bound by the laws of the state in which the registrant was domiciled. It called attention to decisions of courts in other jurisdictions which regarded such donations "as evidence that would raise a presumption of fraud or gross overvaluation sufficient to permit rejection of the directors' valuation."[81] Reference to this diversity of position of courts was, however, only an incident. "With the question of whether or not stock reacquired under these circumstances is true treasury stock and hence is to be regarded as fully paid and non-assessable, this Commission in this case has no concern; but, under the standards of truthfulness demanded by the Securities Act,

---

[80]I Decisions 25.
[81]*Ibid.*, p. 33.

such an entry cannot be regarded as otherwise than untrue and misleading."[82]

The Continental Distillers and Importers Corporation[83] claimed that its fixed assets cost $125,000. The Commission held that this was $50,000 too high; regardless of what the records showed as to the value of the assets the corporation received in exchange for its stock, much of the issue would have to be regarded as payment to the promoters. Although the Commission did not insist that the cost to the corporation should be identical with the cost to the promoters, it did believe the balance sheet should have contained a statement explaining that cost to the corporation was determined by a sale whose terms were dictated by a promoter and that the promoter had been the owner of the property.[84]

In the matter of Breeze Corporations, Inc.,[85] the Commission expressed the belief that "it is the cost of the assets to the enterprise, as distinguished from their cost to the particular corporate entity, which is significant to the prospective investor." Three predecessor corporations had sold certain intangible property to the registrant at prices in advance of original cost. Although the Commission was unwilling to decide "whether the inclusion in the balance sheet of any appreciation in the valuation of the company's intangibles as of the date of its formation would in itself constitute a deficiency," it was nevertheless of the opinion that since the registrant had been established by the per-

---

[82]*Ibid.*, p. 33.
[83]I Decisions 54.
[84]In the *Brandy-Wine Brewing Company Case* (I Decisions 138) the Commission refused to disapprove a valuation figure alleged to represent the cost of property to the promoter. The trial examiner believed that the property had been greatly overvalued, but although the Commission thought the evidence gave strong support to that opinion, it was nevertheless unwilling to accept the trial examiner's view.
[85]III Decisions 709, 727.

sons who controlled its predecessors, failure to include "an additional statement showing to what extent these figures represented write-ups either by the predecessor companies or by the issuer, and the circumstances thereof, was materially misleading."[86]

The Commission has consistently held that the stated value of donated shares should never be reflected in the item of Property. Whatever may be said about donated stock, it must, in the judgment of the Commission, never be used to obscure the truth regarding the value of property. It has also been zealous in its efforts to prevent a padding of the property account when excessive amounts of stock have been given for property and the recipients have been under no obligation to donate portions of it to the corporation. An important method which the Commission has used repeatedly in testing the sincerity of such valuations has been an examination of the record of the prices of a registrant's stock at the time of such purchase of property.

The Virginia City Gold Mining Company[87] had acquired some mining property and equipment for two million shares of stock having a par value of 10c. These properties it valued at $200,000. The record disclosed, however, that thirty per cent of the stock had been returned to the corporation as a gift. This, in the opinion of the Commission, should have resulted in a reduction of $60,000 in the value of the property. Moreover, the stock which had been sold for cash at about the time these units of property were acquired never brought more than 5c a share. The property could not have been worth much more than $70,000 at the time it was acquired, in the judgment of the Commission.

---

[86] *Ibid.*, 728.
[87] II Decisions 855.

Appraisals

"Valuations are, of course, in the final analysis expressions of judgment informed by knowledge and experience. But an appraisal purports to be more than an arbitrary determination of value."[88] Basic in an appraisal are the choice of a method and the correct application of the method. The Commission has not committed itself to the use of any particular method of valuation, but it has been critical of the ways appraisers have used in applying particular methods. Property of the Haddam Distillers Corporation[89] had been appraised at more than three times its cost to promoters. The appraisal company which had been employed by the registrant made use of replacement cost new and "sound value" (replacement cost new minus depreciation) in reaching its estimates of what the property was worth. The Commission had doubt about the efficacy of such methods of valuation when the property had been purchased of promoters who not only had the property to sell but were in position to force the corporation to buy at their price. Although critical of these methods, the Commission found its justification for dissent from the findings of the appraisers not in the methods employed but in the ways the methods had been used. "If the norm chosen be 'replacement cost new,' weight wherever possible must be given to current or averaged market prices in the case of standard materials, and in other situations attention must be directed toward a detailed analysis of construction and estimates of construction based upon experience."[90] These things the appraisal company had not done and its findings were therefore rejected by the Commission.

---

[88] I Decisions 42.
[89] I Decisions 41.
[90] *Ibid.*, p. 42.

The Continental Distillers and Importers Corporation[91] valued at \$22,500 property which had but recently been sold by an earlier owner for \$5,000. This valuation was the result of an appraisal in which the methods of replacement cost new and of so-called sound value were employed. A representative of the appraisal company when asked what effect the presence of a water supply and a railroad siding in the vicinity of the registrant's property had upon the value of that property, replied: "I would say 40% for the water, 40% for the railroad siding, and the remaining 20% to central location, labor supply, and minor influences."[92] Although it is important in distillation to have water of the proper mineral content which is free from "obnoxious smells," nobody had made a chemical analysis of the water supply which entered in such an important way into the valuation of the registrant's property. The Commission would undoubtedly have given consideration to any expert opinion that might have been presented to indicate that the property had unusual qualities differentiating it from other properties in the same vicinity and making it peculiarly adapted to the purposes of the registrant. But no such testimony was presented and the Commission declared that the registrant had not valued its property correctly.[93]

However much variation there may be in the judgment of competent appraisers as to the value of a building site or of an office structure, either of such kinds of property is of such a character as to make physical measurement possible. The problem of measuring the supply of unexplored coal or gold or silver or oil is not so simple, and it has been primarily because of this fact that unpromising oil and mining

---

[91]I Decisions 54.

[92]*Ibid.*, p. 70.

[93]See also the Winnebago Distilling Company case, VI Decisions 930.

companies have been able to play upon the imagination of large numbers of people who have been induced to buy their securities. Since the establishment of the Securities and Exchange Commission, however, it has not been so easy for such organizations to make extravagant claims as to the amount and value of their resources as it had been previously. Methods of estimating the supply and value of such resources have been subjected to severely critical examination by the Commission.

The "doodle bug" method of appraisal is not acceptable. This method is illustrated in the case of La Luz Mining Corporation.[94] The value of the ore resources of this corporation had been determined by a former fruit grower who represented himself to be a qualified geologist and scientist. Equipped with a "mineral indicator" consisting of a short cylinder and a leather thong he was able, according to his testimony, to determine not only the quantity but the quality of gold ore in any given area. His technique was to place himself in varying physical positions and to allow the mineral indicator freedom of oscillation. By keeping a record of the number of movements of the indicator in each position it was possible, he alleged, to determine the approximate shape of the underlying ore. Such a method of valuation was unacceptable to the Commission.

Nor is it any longer possible for a registrant to disregard the simple classification which competent mining engineers employ in defining ore bodies. In estimating the value of its ores it must differentiate among "proven," "probable," and "possible" ores. "Possible ore" cannot be definitely

---

[94] I Decisions 219.

known or stated in any terms of tonnage.[95] "Estimates of proven or blocked-out ore invariably rest upon precise observations, involving measurements and samplings of the exposed portions of the ore bodies."[96] To assure itself that mining companies will not be permitted to make extravagant claims about ores the Commission employs competent mining engineers who are not only available for testimony but who make field studies of mining properties owned by registrants.

It is not enough to be informed about the supply of any mineral; there are variations in the quality of any such product which lead to variations in values. It is appropriate to make use of the process of sampling in arriving at values, but the Commission is interested in the methods that are used in choosing samples. The president of one company[97] interested in coal mining selected his own samples of coal and had them sent to a laboratory for examination. "It is clear," said the Commission, "that the probative value of laboratory analyses made from samples obtained under such circumstances is slight."[98] Samples chosen by the Commission and tested at the Bureau of Mines failed to confirm the registrant's claims regarding the quality of its coal. If sampling is to be used in valuations, it is necessary, moreover, that the number of samples be adequate. In the matter of La Luz Mining Company[99] the Commission was critical of the use of but three samples,

---

[95]Hoover, Principles of Mining. The Instruction Book for Form A-0-1 states that proven ore is to be regarded as "a block of ore so extensively surrounded by sampled faces that the risk of failure in continuity is reduced to a minimum." Probable ore is "ore to which the risk of failure in continuity is greater than for proven ore, but as to which there is sufficient warrant for assuming continuity of the ore."

[96]*Gilpin Eureka Consolidated Mines, Inc.* I Decisions 756.

[97]*American Terminals and Transit Company.* I Decisions 729.

[98]*Ibid.*

[99]I Decisions 217.

when competent engineers were accustomed to samples of a thousand or more units in valuations of large ore deposits.[100]

Mining ventures have been "susceptible to that type of promotional activity which is directed less to the ultimate purpose of exploiting ore deposits than to an immediate purpose of exploiting prospective investors."[101] The Commission may be willing to admit the possible accuracy of a registrant's claim regarding the value of an ore deposit and yet require unmistakable proof that the allegations are well founded. This position is exemplified in the case of the Doris Ruby Mining Company,[102] which included in its registration statement the observation that "these white porphyry dikes have been proven to be the source of gold depositions." An engineer in the employ of the Commission explained that there were "two schools of thought" among members of the mining profession "as to the source of gold depositions" in the region in which the registrant was interested. The company alleged that it possessed rich gold deposits. The Commission, admitting the possibility that this might be true, was of the opinion that the claim had not been proved and "should not have been made the basis of a positive statement."

Appraisals based on prospective earnings received the Commission's attention, very briefly, in the matter of Breese Corporations, Inc. "The estimates of future annual sales," it said, "constitute the keystone of this appraisal. Assuming, without deciding, that in view of this company's actual earnings record, future estimates might be a proper

---

[100]See also *Platoro Gold Mines, Inc.*, III Decisions 872, and *U. S. Chromium, Inc.*, VI Decisions 891.

[101]*Ypres Cadillac Mines Limited.* III Decisions 47.

[102]IV Decisions 427.

basis, in no event could such estimates extend beyond the bounds of 'reasonable expectation.' "[103] Such a statement quite clearly throws no light on what attitude the Commission might take toward appraisals based upon earning power if earnings were reasonably estimated. In a later opinion[104] it dealt with the same problem; it found fault, however, not with the computation of prospective earnings, but with the rate at which the registrant proposed to capitalize estimated earnings. The rate was seven per cent and this the Commission believed to be "far too low as a basis for determining the present value of the registrant's property."

Unrealized appreciation, based upon revaluation of assets, was subjected to examination by the Commission in the Unity Gold Corporation case.[105] At the time of its reorganization the company had its property appraised. The item for Deferred Development was increased by more than one hundred thousand dollars in excess of cost, the new valuation being based solely on cost of reproduction new. The Commission found no fault with either the independence or the ability of the appraiser. Nor did it raise any question as to the claim of the registrant regarding the "cost of reproducing Deferred Development New." The Commission was quite ready to admit that if the company were to reproduce its deferred development, the cost might possibly be equal to the sum represented to be the present worth of that item. But since the registrant had no blocked out ore and since it had shown no profit in more than two years of operation, the "inclusion of this valuation in the balance sheet translates mere future hopes for the success

---

[103] III Decisions 720.

[104] *Monitor Gold Mining Company.* IV Decisions 347.

[105] III Decisions 618. For an earlier experience of the Unity Gold Corporation as a registrant, see I Decisions 25.

of the enterprise into terms of present fact.'' It was, besides, the opinion of certain engineers that ''the development had not been done properly. As a consequence, in the
future this development might even prove to be a disadvantage to the company rather than a benefit. Under these
circumstances the valuation is perforce misleading. It rep-
resents to prospective security holders a present appreciation which in fact is non-existent.''

In some instances tests of reputed values have been made
by comparing them with prices that similarly situated property has brought in recent sales. In one case the records
of real estate sales and of tax appraisals were searched in
vain for evidence to support the registrant's claim that its
unspecialized property had a high value.[106] In another instance the registrant offered support for its valuation of
coal land by calling attention to prices which coal land
located near at hand had brought in earlier sales.[107] The
Commission challenged this basis of comparison, however,
because the lands had been sold many years earlier at a
time when there was a shortage of coal and they had a
proximity to the market which the registrant did not have.
Supporting a valuation by reference to the recent record of
prices obtained for similarly situated property would evidently have the approval of the Commission. Comparison
is impossible, however, in the absence of substantial similarity of facts. In yet another case the Commission com-
mented upon the difficulty of arriving ''at any precise valuation for such a highly speculative venture as a lode mine
possessing no proven ore. Any valuation must be based
largely upon the good faith of the parties. But relevant to
any such valuation is the evidence as to what experienced

---

[106]*Continental Distillers and Importers Corporation.* I Decisions 54.
[107]*American Terminals and Transit Company.* I Decisions 717.

speculators were willing to give or take for the property.''[108]

Even where facts are known, it is possible to utilize the wrong methods of summarization and hence give a distorted report of values. In the case of Gilpin Eureka Consolidated Mines, Inc.,[109] the Commission was critical of the use of the arithmetical method of averaging for the purpose of finding the average value of gold per ton of ore. In its prospectus the registrant reported upon certain shipments it had made in the past: 11 tons at a value of $47.37 per ton; 1 ton at a value of $213.74 per ton; 10 tons at a value of $16.28 per ton. Summarizing and dividing by 3, it concluded that the average value was $92.46. The Commission, dissenting from this method of averaging, contended that the only fair way of reaching average value would be to use a weighted method. By multiplying the number of tons in each shipment by the reported value per ton, summarizing the results and dividing by the total number of tons, the resulting average is $40.70 a ton.

Finally, the validity of an appraisal depends upon how its results are to be used. The Mining and Development Corporation[110] had valued its ore resources on the basis of an estimate made by a mining engineer. His valuation ''had been reached by deducting estimated operating costs from the total gross estimated recoverable value.'' There was no evidence that the engineer intended to make an appraisal to be used in connection with the sale of securities. In any event he did not take account of the fact that the mine could have a life of no more than a very few years; nor did he, therefore, undertake to estimate the present worth of the

---

[108] *Unity Gold Corporation.* I Decisions 35.
[109] I Decisions 752.
[110] I Decisions 786, 797.

aggregate expected profit.[111] The estimate was valid for operating purposes, in the judgment of an expert in mining engineering who represented the Commission, but unsatisfactory for the purpose of determining the value of property for the information of prospective owners of registrant's securities.

Thus far the discussion of valuation has related to physical property exclusively. The attitude of the Commission toward the valuation of intangibles will be illustrated by brief reference to patent rights. The most elementary interest of the Commission in patent rights is in the validity of the claims of registrants as to the existence of such rights. Although it would be difficult for the Commission to search the records of the patent office to verify all claims of the existence of patent rights, every well informed registrant knows that its claims may possibly be subjected to such a test. Lewis American Airways, Inc.,[112] claimed to have certain patents and to have filed application for others. Examination of the patent office records disclosed the falsity of these claims.

Although the Commission was quite critical of the method used by this registrant in dealing with patents, it did nothing more with the problem of valuation than to suggest that whenever there is a purely arbitrary valuation of patents, the accountant ought to say so frankly. A year and a half later it dealt somewhat more seriously with the problem. An appraiser had valued the patent applications of the Petersen Engine Company, Inc.[113] He finally admit-

---

[111]Appraisals of ore properties are likely to be condemned by the Commission if the appraisers have neglected to estimate the present worth of anticipated income. See especially *La Luz Mining Corporation*, I Decisions 223; *American Terminal and Transit Company*, I Decisions 719; and *Mining and Development Corporation*, I Decisions 797.

[112]I Decisions 330.

[113]II Decisions 893.

ted to the Commission that his estimate had been purely arbitrary and had been reached as a result of sheer guesswork. With apparent approval the Commission quoted one of its own engineers who declared that there are four accepted bases for valuing a patent. They are: "(1) the amount of an actual cash sale between parties dealing at arms length with each other; (2) the amount of a bona fide cash offer to purchase made by a financially responsible person; (3) a capitalization of the royalties obtained from a patent; and (4) a capitalization of those earnings of a company that were strictly attributable to a patent."[114]

Many registrants have represented their appraisers as expert valuation engineers. Sunset Gold Fields, Inc.,[115] for example, presented a report from a man who used letterheads containing his name, his address, and the words *engineering and surveying*. The average uninformed investor would probably regard such a person as being a mining engineer, but he was not. He had had some training in electrical engineering but had not finished an engineering course. Prior to the time he became interested in the registrant he had been manager of a hotel and was chosen to act as engineer merely because "some form of engineer's report was desirable in connection with the registration statement." He happened to be one of the entrepreneurs, but the fact that he had an interest in the company was of no importance to the Commission in rejecting his report, except that his financial interest helped to confirm the Commission's judgment that "he was not hired in the first instance because of any engineering talent he may have had."[116]

---

[114]II Decisions 907.
[115]II Decisions 329.
[116]*Ibid.*, p. 333.

Although accountants who certify financial statements must be completely independent, a different standard applies in the case of engineers. A registrant is not required "to file a report by an independent engineer,"[117] but it is expected to "disclose to the investors all the material facts concerning the relationship between the engineer and the company."[118]

The Commission has never expressed itself better upon the matter of experts than when it said:

"The qualifications which characterize the expert are not rigid and categorical. Certainly, training, integrity, intelligence and experience are among them. We do not attempt to present a precise scale for the measurement of these qualifications. It is equally certain, however, that one who is truly an expert brings to his work knowledge and skill which are the substance of his profession and which are evinced by his use of the principles and procedures normal to others in his field, and we can and do take the position that, by the failure to employ such normal principles and procedures, the absence of the requisite knowledge and skill is disclosed."[119]

Summing up the position of the Commission with reference to valuation, it may be said that in attempting to discover the genuine cost of property it has been obliged to penetrate many subterfuges. It has had to judge the validity of claims as to cost by studying the recent history of ownership of property for the purpose of learning whether promoters, or directors, officers or principal stockholders profited from its sale to the issuer. In addition to any such direct information as this, it has often concluded that figures for cost have been unreliable when portions of par value stock given for property have been returned to the corporation as a gift without any proportionate reduction in the value of property and when property which has been

[117]II Decisions 153.
[118]*Ibid.*
[119]*Gilpin Eureka Consolidated Mines, Inc.* I Decisions 757, 758.

obtained in exchange for stock is carried at an amount equal to the par value of such stock even though the market value of the stock at the time of the transaction happened to be less than par.

The Commission is not committed to any theory with respect to appraisals. It does insist that the theory which is adopted must be adequate to the requirements of the particular situation. Replacement cost, less depreciation, has very little validity, for example, when it yields a figure considerably larger than the price at which the property was but recently purchased by the promoter. It is insistent, too, that once a defensible theory of valuation has been chosen for use in any given situation, all of the factors necessary for giving the theory effect must be considered by the appraiser. It is not necessary, finally, that an independent engineer's report be filed. If the engineer has an interest in the registrant, and if that fact is set forth frankly, the report will be accepted, provided the engineer who made it is able to qualify as an expert.[120]

---

[120]But in some cases independent engineers are required under the Trust Indenture Act. See pages 84 and 85.

CHAPTER VII

UNDERWRITERS SINCE 1933

"The term 'underwriter' means any person who has purchased from an issuer with a view to, or sells for an issuer in connection with, the distribution of any security, or participates or has a direct or indirect participation in any such undertaking, or participates or has a participation in the direct or indirect underwriting of any such undertaking; but such term shall not include a person whose interest is limited to a commission from an underwriter or dealer not in excess of the usual and customary distributors' or sellers' commission. As used in this paragraph the term 'issuer' shall include, in addition to an issuer, any person directly or indirectly controlling or controlled by the issuer, or any person under direct or indirect common control with the issuer.'"[1]

INTERPRETATION OF THE DEFINITION

It is only rarely that the Commission is obliged to rule that persons represented to be underwriters are to be classified otherwise. Such a ruling occurred in the case of the Commonwealth Bond Corporation, Inc.,[2] an organization which acted as the protective committee for the mortgage bondholders of the Tudor Corporation. The registration statement reported the Commonwealth as the principal underwriter, but the Commission decided that a reorganiza-

---

[1] Securities Act, Section 2(11).
[2] I Decisions 13.

195

tion committee, even though it acted as the underwriter for bonds originally issued by the corporation, is not to be regarded as an underwriter within the meaning of that word as it is used in the Securities Act.

Sometimes corporations handle for themselves the marketing of securities that they issue. In all such cases it would obviously be impossible for selling to occur without the help of officers and employees, and yet it would hardly seem reasonable to classify these persons as underwriters. In the matter of Free Traders, Inc.,[3] the Commission, dealing with a case in which directors proposed "to sell shares to friends and acquaintances," expressed the view that "determination of the question whether a director or officer aiding in the distribution of a security is acting as an officer of the issuer or is acting individually as an underwriter depends upon a variety of facts and circumstances in each particular case. Upon the facts disclosed by this record, we cannot say that any of the directors . . . proposes to sell otherwise than as an officer of the company."[4]

Issuers have sometimes refused to disclose the identity of underwriters either because they have desired to keep investors from knowing their names or because of a misconception as to who should be regarded as underwriters. Illustrative of the latter is the case of the Kinner Airplane and Motor Corporation, Ltd.[5] The Commission believed that the president of the company should have been reported as an underwriter. The issuer replied that inasmuch as there had been no firm commitment there was no under-

---

[3] S.E.C., Securities Act Release No. 2312, August 1, 1940.

[4] *Ibid.*, p. 8. *In the Matter of the American Tung Grove Developments, Inc.*, however, the Commission ruled that certain officers who expected to "spend a major part of their time and efforts in the sale of registrant's securities" would have to be classified as underwriters. Securities Act Release 2361, September 30, 1940.

[5] II Decisions 943,

writing contract. The Commission responded that commitments are not necessary to give a person the status of an underwriter; that plans for the distribution of securities at the time a registration statement became effective may be inferred by an examination in retrospect of what occurred after the process of distribution began. The examination in this case revealed that the president, during a period of but little more than two years, had sold in excess of a quarter of a million shares of the registrant's stock. The corporation further attempted to justify the omission of the name of the president as an underwriter by calling attention to the fact that he, as an officer and director, had signed the registration statement and thus committed himself to all the liabilities of the Securities Act as completely as though he had signed as an underwriter besides. It was of the opinion that "the only purpose of defining an 'underwriter' in the Securities Act appears to be to fix the civil liability of such an individual or concern in case of falsity in the registration statement."[6] From this narrow conception the Commission dissented, expressing the view that queries upon underwriting were "designed to bring out not only the existence of underwriting and the identity of the underwriters but also the control relationship, if any, existing between the issuer and underwriters, and the terms of the underwriting and distribution."[7]

The Commission found that the underwriters for Sweet's Steel Company had not been correctly named.[8] One of the organizations which did not wish to have itself named as an underwriter had entered into a contract which required it to accept 3028 shares of the registrant's stock as collat-

---

[6] *Ibid.,* 948.

[7] *Ibid.,* 948.

[8] IV Decisions 589. See also the *Reiter-Foster Oil Corporation case,* VI Decisions 1028.

eral for a loan of $302,800. As stock was sold it was to be delivered by the organization which held it as collateral. In the meantime the unnamed enterprise was to receive "all dividends and other rights pertaining to the ownership of the shares," and when the account was finally closed it was to have a substantial sum as compensation for its services. The Commission did not believe that this contract possessed the "normal attributes of a loan or pledge."

The liabilities enumerated in the law[9] relate to transactions for which the underwriter is responsible during the period of distribution. When that process is completed, the status of the underwriter changes.[10] The underwriter who conducts transactions in securities one year after they were originally offered, provided the distribution was completed within that year, ceases to be an underwriter and becomes a dealer.

If a purchaser of securities buys for purposes of investment rather than distribution, that purchase does not involve underwriting even though there may be an agreement to absorb unsold portions of the issue at the end of the period of public distribution. If the buyer is to be exempted from being classified as an underwriter, it is neces-

---

[9]Since 1934 the liability of the underwriter has been limited to the total amount at which securities distributed by him were sold to the public.

[10]This conclusion rests upon a statement in the House Committee Report on the Securities Act and an observation of the Commission. The House Committee said: "Transactions by an underwriter are not exempted. It is true, however, that there is a point of time when a person who has become an underwriter ceases to exercise any underwriting function and, therefore, ceases to be an underwriter. When that point is reached such a person would be subject only to whatever restrictions would be imposed upon him as a dealer." (H. R. Report 85, 73rd Congress, 1st Session, p. 16.)

The Commission commenting upon the "presumption that sales by dealers within a period of one year . . . are a part of the distribution of the issue," has expressed the belief that this is not "a conclusive presumption of law" but a "presumption of fact subject to refutation upon a showing of fact that distribution was completed within less than one year." *Brooklyn Manhattan Transit Corporation*, I Decisions 162-163.

sary, however, that there be no community of interest with the issuer or any underwriter and that there be no "privity of contract with the issuer."[11]

Whether purchases are made for investment solely must be determined, in the judgment of the General Counsel, "by reference to the intention of the purchaser at the time of purchase."[12] It is conceivable that a purchase might be made for purposes of investment and that some circumstance would arise within a few hours which would justify the buyer in changing his mind. In attempting to decide, however, whether the purchase in any such case was actually made for investment the purchaser's conduct may be of much greater "significance than his statements in throwing light on what his state of mind was at a given time."

Important among the items of evidence throwing light upon the purchaser's state of mind are the length of time elapsing between purchase and sale and the character of the purchaser's business. If as much as a year elapses before sale occurs, the purchase was made presumptively for investment, but it is conceivable that there might have been a plan to wait for a year to complete the distribution, in which case the purchaser would have to be regarded as an underwriter. It would be more difficult for dealers in securities or investment banks to prove that purchases were for investment than would be the case if the purchasers happened to be insurance or investment companies, for the customary business of the former is distribution of securities whereas the latter are interested in ownership of securities rather than distribution.

---

[11]Rule 142, Securities Act.
[12]S.E.C. Securities Act Release 1861, December 13, 1938.

INDEPENDENCE

The Commission has manifested great interest in the independence of underwriters. If the underwriter controls or is controlled by the issuer directly or indirectly, that fact should be revealed to investors in order that they may better judge the fairness of the underwriting spread. Without scrutiny by the Commission the relationship between the issuer and the underwriter would never be apparent to the casual investor in such a case as that involving the Equity Corporation and Allied Distributors, Inc.[13] Equity Corporation reported that there was no underwriter which it controlled or by which it was controlled. The Commission discovered, however, that although the underwriter was not controlled directly by the issuer the interrelationship between "the parent of the underwriter, and various corporations affiliated with the registrant . . . was such as to indicate that the underwriter and issuer were controlled by the same parties."[14]

FITNESS

The Commission has been interested in making inquiry into the financial responsibility of underwriters as well as the quality of their previous experience. If an underwriter is without financial responsibility, the distribution may be only partially successful. Those who buy upon the expec-

---

[13] II Decisions 675.

[14] *Ibid.*, 681. In earlier parts of this discussion repeated references have been made to the opinion of the Commission in the Equity Corporation case. At the close of the opinion there is a separate statement by Commissioner Healy which reads in part: "I cannot resist commenting upon the bewildering maze of corporations involved in the transactions described and upon the labyrinthic course of the transactions themselves among these artificial beings, these corporate slaves, called into existence by those who move them about and control them more completely than ever a master ordered the lives and acts of human slaves." *Ibid.*, p. 689.

tation that all securities will be sold may find that the funds they provide are insufficient to meet the needs of the issuer and that the value of their investment accordingly declines. The National Boston Montana Mines Corporation[15] declared in its registration statement that the underwriter was prepared to buy for cash. This the Commission found to be false because the underwriter "was known to be without funds or credit."[16]

The principal underwriter for Bering Straits Tin Mines, Inc.,[17] represented to the registrant that it had contacts with "many excellent investment banking firms throughout the United States and Canada"; that these contacts had been in the process of development for over a quarter of a century. It reported to the issuer that "several tentative contracts have been made with Eastern brokers relative to handling your issue." A few days after the statement became effective, however, the underwriter advised the issuer that it had decided to withdraw from participation in the distribution. In the meantime stop order proceedings had been initiated by the Commission. As a result of subsequent inquiry it developed that the president of the registrant had been deceived by the provisions of the underwriting contract; that the underwriter had "apparently made no effort to contact any retail dealers for the sale of registrant's shares";[18] that its previous experience in the distribution of securities had been entirely unsuccessful.

COMMITMENTS

What the character of the contract between an underwriter and issuer may be is unimportant so long as it is

---

[15]II Decisions 226.　　[17]II Decisions 486.
[16]*Ibid.*, 247.　　　　 [18]*Ibid.*, 492.

described with clarity and without dissimulation.[19]   The Livingston Mining Company[20] had not told the truth, in the judgment of the Commission, regarding its underwriting agreement.   Correctly stating the price to be paid by the underwriter for its shares and the total number of shares to be sold, it left the impression that there was a firm commitment whereas the underwriter merely had an option to buy the shares; that he expected to sell as many of them as possible; and that the corporation could obtain the sum of money represented as constituting the expected proceeds of the sale, only provided all the shares were actually sold.

The Callahan Zinc-Lead Company[21] had an underwriting agreement which provided that it would attempt the distribution of its shares among its shareholders on the basis of their preemptive right with the assurance that the underwriters would take up the shares that were not thus subscribed for.   The contract would have permitted the underwriters to make payment in yet to be identified property or securities at prices subject to determination in the future.   The existing stockholders would have been required to pay a dollar a share for the stock.   Inasmuch as it was selling in the market at seventy-five cents a share, it was to be expected that the underwriters would be required to accept the whole new issue.   The New York Stock Exchange, on which the outstanding issue was listed, announced that it would not allow the listing of the new stock unless the underwriting contract was abrogated and the stock offered only to stockholders.   To have allowed execution of the original plan would have opened the way for

---

[19]Unless there are firm commitments pro forma balance sheets showing anticipated proceeds from the sale of the proposed issue are not permitted.   I Decisions 53, 78.

[20]II Decisions 141.

[21]I Decisions 115.

the sale of the proposed issue at what might have been an inequitably low price.

The Securities Act imposed new risks upon investment bankers. Not only did they become subject to suits if they participated in the distribution of securities on the basis of false or misleading information; if they made firm commitments, they could never be sure what disturbing situation might arise in the financial markets to handicap them in disposing of securities for which a registration statement was yet to become effective. The best remedy that banks have found for the risks of the waiting period is for them to combine at the outset in purchasing securities. Whereas it was once the practice for an issuer to enter into a contract with a single bank, it is now customary for several banks to sign a contract for a single issue if it is of considerable size. The originator, in the old sense, still conducts preliminary investigations and negotiations, but the actual risks are distributed from the beginning among the purchasers who are associated with the originator. Shortly after the Securities Act became effective it was customary for underwriters to limit firm commitments by a hedge in their contracts which gave them power to cancel agreements under certain conditions and for specified reasons. Sometimes cancellation might occur at any time before a statement became effective; sometimes cancellation might occur at a later time but not after the original public distribution got under way.[22] Although there was a subsequent decline in

---

[22]A characteristic *market clause* provided that the agreement might be terminated if ''any substantial change in the financial position of your company or any subsidiary, or in the existing operating, political, economic or market conditions shall have taken place, which, in the judgment of _____ & Company as the representative of the Underwriting Group with the concurrence of underwriters who, together with it, have agreed to purchase not less than 50% of the aggregate principal amount of the Bonds, renders it impracticable or inadvisable to market the Bonds at the price to the public named in paragraph _____.''

the use of hedge clauses, they are "nevertheless much more widely employed in bond financing than was the case prior to the Act."[23]

SPREADS

There must be adequate publicity as to the amount of the spread. It is the judgment of Gourrich that spreads for bonds are now lower than they were before the Securities Act became effective. He reports that before 1933 they averaged approximatly three or four per cent of par (spreads on preferred stock averaged five per cent of par), whereas spreads on bonds after security selling began to increase in 1935 "declined to less than 2¼% of par." As for preferred stock, the average on "eighteen such issues sold during 1935 and 1936" was "about 4¼% of the public offering price."[24] It is possible that a part, or perhaps all, of this decline has been the result of the Securities Act, which because of enforced publicity provides issuers with a basis for learning what other organizations pay for investment banking services and which puts investors on guard against issues providing underwriters excessive spreads. Gourrich admits that the offerings of underwriters since 1933 have been restricted largely to securities of high investment quality which could be distributed without great outlay for salesmanship. It is possible, besides, that some of the outlays which otherwise would have been borne by bankers in preparing an issue for sale have been met by

---

[23]Paul F. Gourrich, "Investment Banking Methods Prior to and Since the Securities Act of 1933," *Law and Contemporary Problems*, Jan., 1937, p. 3.

[24]*Ibid.*, p. 70. On page 3 of a study entitled *Cost of Flotation for Registered Securities, 1938-1939* (published March, 1941), the Commission says that "distributors averaged 2.0 percent for underwritten bonds, 5.1 percent for underwritten preferred stock, 14.9 percent for non-underwritten preferred stock, 15.1 percent for underwritten common stock, and 17.3 percent for non underwritten common."

issuers. If so, a lower spread would not of necessity indicate a reduction in the net outlay for underwriters' services.

MARKETING

The Securities Act has resulted in no significant change in the general plan for the actual process of marketing. It has come to be customary for "red herring" prospectuses to be sent to dealers two or three days before a registration statement becomes effective in order that those who are to be asked to participate in selling groups may be informed as to the issue they will be given an opportunity to sell. This preliminary "prospectus" contains information which the bankers regard as being salient. The complete prospectus meeting the requirements of the Commission for public distribution becomes available to dealers at the end of the waiting period. As soon as a statement becomes effective, contracts are submitted to dealers who have been included in the selling group. Numerous banks, in fact, have engaged the Western Union to accept for preliminary delivery to its offices throughout the country letters containing contracts, addressed to prospective members of selling groups, to be put in local post offices one minute after midnight on the first day that securities may be sold.[25]

The waiting period has been very unpopular with bankers. Although it is illegal for them to accept orders, however tentative, until statements become effective, it is widely recognized that many of them have been guilty of "beating the gun." It is difficult to see how it can ever be otherwise, for it is the policy of the Commission to encourage distribu-

---

[25]The Commission modified its Securities Act Rule 930 on July 18, 1939. In order to accommodate those who wish to advertise issues in the early morning papers of the effective date of a registration it is provided that the statement shall bcome effective 19 full periods of 24 hours each subsequent to half past four in the afternoon of the date of filing. Securities Act Release 2016.

tion of informative literature prior to the period of distribution, with the single limitation that nothing which is done might be construed as an offer to buy or an offer to sell. There is no way, however, to prevent gentlemen's agreements which in some instances may be so nebulous as to involve understandings which are not expressed in words. The objections to the waiting period are based upon the underwriter's fear of an unfavorable change in the market.

Although the general scheme of syndication is not substantially different from what it was during the flourishing period of investment banking, there is not as much shifting of title to securities as there once was. For this the Securities Act is not responsible, however. Transfer taxes have encouraged members of purchase groups to retain ownership of that portion of an issue which they expect to sell. Without transfer taxes it would obviously be more economical at present to shift securities from one group to another and back again if such shifting seemed desirable.

The market is not supported during the period of primary distribution as extensively as it once was. This is to be explained in part on the ground that the securities which have been floated since 1933 have, on the whole, possessed investment quality of such an attractive character that support has been unnecessary. The restrictions upon pegging and stabilizing activities have, moreover, modified substantially the character of market control which once prevailed. Not only is it difficult, in many instances impossible, to organize a market during the period of primary distribution, through use of the facilities of exchanges; the prohibition against "pegging, fixing or stabilizing the price of such security in contravention of such rules and regulations as the Commission may prescribe as necessary or appropriate in the public interest or for the protection of investors''[26] has been a restraining influence.

Although support of the market has ceased to have great significance in primary distribution, "pegging, fixing and stabilizing" continues to be the policy of underwriters engaged in secondary distributions; that is, sales, through the use of investment banks, of large blocks of securities that may have been outstanding for long periods and sales of unsold portions of issues whose original distribution was not finished at the termination of the period during which selling groups existed.

Canusa Gold Mines[27] stated that it expected to sell its stock at prices prevailing from day to day in the over-the-counter markets of Toronto and Detroit. This was apparently strictly true but insufficient, nevertheless, in the judgment of the Commission, for the market in which sales were to occur was not one in which there was free play of demand and supply. The underwriter had manipulated the market; prices of the stock had been subject to wide and sudden changes. During the month within which the registration statement became effective the high price of the stock was sixty per cent higher than its low. An important part of the plan for rigging the market had been the withdrawal of over three hundred and fifty thousand shares of the stock which the directors and certain principal stockholders placed in escrow on terms which forbade its release to anyone except the underwriter.

Early in 1935 the president of Otis and Company, an investment banking house in Cleveland, came to the conclusion that the stock of the Murray-Ohio Company was "being offered below its intrinsic value and that its selling price

---

[26]Securities Exchange Act 9(a)(6).
[27]II Decisions 548.

would soon reflect the marked improvement in the company's economic condition.''[28] Sixty thousand shares of stock of the company were outstanding and approximately half of it was in the possession of a small number of persons. Otis and Company purchased 4918 shares from five of the large stockholders at $10.50 a share with the understanding that the sellers would not offer any of the shares which they continued to own, until after the expiration of a period of sixty days. During that period Otis and Company expected to redistribute at a profit to itself the shares that it had purchased. Its salesmen and customers were provided with literature which stated that Murray-Ohio stock was ''an attractive speculation at current price levels'' and that ''higher earnings for the company . . . should affect the market price accordingly.'' The stock was made available for purchase ''at the market.''

When the Securities and Exchange Commission learned that the market had not been free and open[29] it obtained an injunction against further violation of the Securities Act. On appeal the injunction was sustained by the Circuit Court of Appeals, which remarked that the ''offer to sell 'at the market' must have been understood to imply a price fixed by supply and demand free from artificial restrictions and

---

[28]*Otis and Company vs. Securities Exchange Commission*, U. S. Circuit Court of Appeals for the Sixth District, September 18, 1939.

[29]The stock of Murray-Ohio was listed on the Cleveland Stock Exchange. From May 9, 1935, to November 20, 1935, its price advanced from 4½ to 19. Contributing to this advance was the fact that several thousand shares had been withheld during the sixty day period ending with August 26. Important, too, was the fact that during that same period 91% of all the shares sold through the facilities of the Cleveland Exchange had been purchased by Otis and Company. During September, October, and November it bought 62% of the shares offered for sale. On November 18, 1935, the Commission began its investigation and two days later Otis and Company ceased buying Murray-Ohio stock.

intentional stimulation at least as far as (Otis and Company) was concerned.''[30]

The Commission has approached the problem of regulating stabilizing activities in a spirit of great caution. Because of differences of opinion as between over-the-counter dealers and those operating through the facilities of securities exchanges with regard to the type of control that should be instituted, the Commission has dealt with the problem only tentatively. It allows stabilizing, but regulates the price range within which stabilizing activities may take place. No purchase for the purpose of stabilizing may occur unless the price paid is within one point of the first purchase made, nor may any price paid be in excess of 102½% of the original purchase. No purchase may be made at a price in excess of the last sale nor may it be made at the price of the last sale unless the "highest price which the security attained on that exchange on the date of the purchase exceeds such last sale price by ½ of 1% of the highest price or ¼ point, whichever is greater.''[31]

Although issuers are free to sell their securities in the market for what they will bring, provided the market is free, the Commission looks with great disfavor on "step up" prices. The Snow Point Mining Company, Inc.,[32] proposed to increase the price of its shares from one dollar to two dollars a share as the number of shares sold increased. The Commission believed that this was nothing but a selling scheme; that salesmen could claim that the assets of the company were increasing and hence could justify an advance in price. Nothing which the company had done or planned to do could support such a possible argument in

[30]*Ibid.*
[31]S.E.C., Securities Exchange Act Release No. 2363, January 3, 1940.
[32]I Decisions 311.

the judgment of the Commission and hence the statement was declared to be false and misleading.

A similar situation was presented in the case of the Avocalon Extension Syndicate, Ltd.[33] Quoting from the statement of the trial examiner with apparent approval the Commission said: "Whatever may be true in other cases, if the registrant announces step-up prices and gives reasons which constitute a one-sided statement of what is in reality a two-sided situation—for the property may turn out to be either more valuable or less valuable than anticipated—then a statement which is entirely true as far as it goes may be so inadequate as to be misleading to at least some prospective purchasers."[34]

---

[33] I Decisions 657.
[34] *Ibid.*, 659.

CHAPTER VIII

THE RESPONSIBILITIES OF ACCOUNTANTS

No person may certify such financial statements as are required under the Securities Act unless he is "duly registered and in good standing."[1] Nor will the Commission recognize an accountant as "independent who is not in fact independent." The Commission explains that an accountant will not be considered independent with respect to any person in whom he has any substantial interest, direct or indirect, or with whom he is, or was during the period of report, connected as a promoter, underwriter, voting trustee, director, officer, or employee."[2]

THE ROLE OF THE ACCOUNTANT

The position of an accountant who owns an interest in the company whose statements he certifies is very well illustrated in the case of the accountant who certified statements for Rickard Ramore Gold Mines, Ltd.[3] This company was authorized to issue three million shares of which some two million were outstanding at the time of the filing of the registration statement, on the basis of which the corporation proposed to sell the remaining authorized but unissued

---

[1]Rule 2-01(a), Regulation S-X. See National Electric Company case for illustration of how the Commission dealt with a certificate signed by an accountant who falsely alleged that he was a C.P.A. S.E.C. Securities Act Release No. 2387, November 6, 1940.
[2]Rule 2-01(b), Regulation S-X.
[3]II Decisions 377.

shares. The certifying accountant owned eleven thousand of the outstanding shares, ten thousand of which he had obtained for accounting services rendered in connection with the original organization of the company. Although the accountant's status as a shareholder was of negligible importance, the Commission held that he could not be regarded as independent because he "would be apt to approach its accounting problems as a stockholder rather than as an independent accountant."[4] His certification was unacceptable to the Commission.

Whether an accountant approaches his responsibilities from the point of view of a stockholder or of the management must depend upon his state of mind which may or may not be colored by the fact that he is a stockholder. The Commission has evidently felt that the test of independence applied in the Rickard Ramore Gold Mines case is not completely definitive, for the following year it hinted that the relationship between the accountant's investment in a company and his total fortune might be taken into consideration in the application of standards of independence. In the second release in its Accounting Series it reported upon a recent opinion in which it held that a firm of accountants was not independent because the value of the holdings of one of the partners in the firm "was substantial and constituted more than one per cent of the partner's personal fortune."[5] It is only by implication that it suggests willingness to disregard the ownership of stock as a test of independence if the amount of an accountant's personal fortune which is invested in the stock of a registrant is almost infinitesimally small. There does not appear to be any

---

[4] *Ibid.*, 389. See also the case of A. Hollander and Son, Inc., S.E.C., Securities Exchange Act Release No. 2777.

[5] Accounting Series Number 2, May 6, 1937.

published record indicating the willingness of the Commission to accept certification by an accountant who owns stock in a registrant in which he has invested less than one per cent of his fortune.

The Accountant as an Employee

The Cornucopia Gold Mines[6] filed a registration containing financial statements which had been certified by a firm of accountants whose independence the Commission challenged. In the employ of this firm was an accountant who was comptroller of the registrant and as such signed its statement as its principal financial officer. Although he was a stockholder and officer of the registrant, he received no compensation for the services he rendered to it as comptroller. He nevertheless had charge of its accounting and as an employee of the firm of accountants was thus in the position of ''reviewing his own work.''[7] It is ''unreasonable to suppose,'' said the Commission in commenting upon the accountant's relationship to the registrant as officer and stockholder, ''that he could cast aside these relationships and view the accounting problems with the objectivity of an 'independent' accountant criticizing and correcting accounting practices and methods of the corporation's own staff.''[8] Not only was the comptroller disqualified as an independent accountant; the Commission was unwilling that the firm with which he was identified should be given an independent status, for it had a contract with the registrant which not only provided that it should be rewarded for its services with a fixed sum of cash but it was to receive ''one per cent of the gross proceeds of the metal sales.''[9] This,

---

[6] I Decisions 364.   [8] *Ibid.*, 366.
[7] *Ibid.*, 366.   [9] *Ibid.*, 367.

in the judgment of the Commission, was "substantial and material continuing pecuniary interest. The holder of such a claim has too close an identity with the financial destinies and too intimate personal concern with the managerial policies of the enterprise to bring to bear . . . the objectivity which is the essence of an 'independent' accountant."[10]

The Accountant Under Domination of the Registrant

The accountant for the Metropolitan Personal Loan Company[11] thought that a reserve which was reported was adequate merely "because the registrant's officers told him so."[12] Other items were included in the financial statements because the officers of the company had demanded that they appear.

"He who, as a result of connivance with, or loyalty or subservience to his client, purposely or recklessly misrepresents the facts, cannot be said to qualify as an 'independent' expert. Protection of investors in these situations requires not only that these fiduciaries be free of the entangling alliances which relational and contractual connections with registrants frequently engender, but also that they approach their task with complete objectivity—critical of the practices and procedures of registrants, and unwilling to aid and abet in making statements which the facts do not warrant."[13]

In response to an inquiry as to whether an accountant who has been guaranteed indemnification against loss is to be regarded as independent, the Chief Accountant of the Commission has said:

"When an accountant and his client, directly or through an affiliate, have entered into an agreement of indemnity which seeks to assure to the accountant immunity from liability for his own negligent acts, whether of omission or commission, it is my opinion

---

[10]*Ibid.*, 367.
[11]II Decisions 803.
[12]*Ibid.*, 813.
[13]*American Terminals and Transit Company*, I Decisions 707.

that one of the major stimuli to objective and unbiased consideration of the problems encountered in a particular engagement is removed or greatly weakened. Such condition must frequently induce a departure from the standards of objectivity and impar-
tiality which the concept of independence implies. In such difficult matters, for example, as the determination of the scope of
audit necessary, existence of such an agreement may easily lead
to the use of less extensive or thorough procedures than would
otherwise be followed. In other cases it may result in a failure
to appraise with professional acumen the information disclosed
by the examination. Consequently, on the basis of the facts set
forth in your inquiry, it is my opinion that the accountant cannot be recognized as independent for the purpose of certifying the
financial statements of the corporation.''[14]

ACCOUNTANTS' CERTIFICATES

An important part of the Commission's program for winning the support, sometimes, apparently, the unwilling support, of the accounting profession is its insistence upon
adequacy of statement in the certificates which accompany
balance sheets and profit and loss statements. The Commission has never prescribed any form for use in certifica-
tions, for it has been considerably less interested in formality than in the integrity of the certificates, adequacy of
statement as to the scope of audits, expressions of opinion
as to the respectability of accounting practices, and any
modifications which should be made in registrants' balance
sheets or profit and loss statements in order to make the
records conform to results that would have occurred had
accepted accounting principles been employed.

The certificate of the independent public accountant employed by the American Terminals and Transit Company[15]
was declared to be inaccurate. The accountant had certified that the financial statements were "true and correct

---

[14]S.E.C., Accounting Series Release No. 22, March 14, 1941.
[15]I Decisions 701.

copies,'' but he admitted in testimony taken by the Commission that the item of cash appearing in the balance sheet was non-existent. Although a certificate may be accurate as of the date on which it was signed, and this presumably will be at least a day or two before a statement is filed with the Commission, changes may take place in the affairs of the registrant which will make the certificate inaccurate before the statement becomes effective. If such changes do occur, it is the responsibility of the accountant to bring them to the attention of the Commission.[16]

The honest accountant may be required or at least feel obliged to disclose the effect of ''extraordinary circumstances occurring between the stated date of the balance sheet and the date of certification.''[17] It is not ordinarily the duty of accountants to undertake prognostications, but in the judgment of the Commission they ''should adopt a liberal attitude towards the problem and make appropriate disclosures, even though in an individual case the clear necessity therefor might not appear.''[18]

Scope of the Audit

The word audit has no uniformity of meaning. To the casual investor who knows but little about accounting it may imply, invariably, a thoroughgoing examination and verification of every item in a financial statement. Its significance is to be determined only in the light of the requirements of a particular assignment. The scope of the audit

[16]S.E.C., Securities Act Release No. 324, March 28, 1935.

[17]*Potrero Sugar Company*, V Decisions 982, 997.

[18]The Commission, recognizing the controversial nature of this issue, supports its position by referring to D. L. Trouant, *Financial Audits* (1937), pp. 178-180; *Proceedings Before the American Institute of Accountants* (1937), pp. 313-318; William H. Bell and John A. Powelson, *Auditing* (1924), p. 341; Robert H. Montgomery, *Auditing Theory and Practice*, 5th edition (1934), pp. 667-669.

has received the attention of the Commission in two different directions. In the first place it has demanded of accountants comprehensive statements in their own language as to the extent of their audits.

"The accountant's certificate (I) shall contain a reasonably comprehensive statement as to the scope of the audit made including, if with respect to significant items in the financial statements any auditing procedures generally recognized as normal have been omitted, a specific designation of such procedures and of the reasons for their omission; (II) shall state whether the audit was made in accordance with generally accepted auditing standards applicable in the circumstances; and (III) shall state whether the audit made omitted any procedure deemed necessary by the accountant under the circumstances of the particular case.

"In determining the scope of the audit necessary, appropriate consideration shall be given to the adequacy of the system of internal check and control. Due weight may be given to an internal system of audit regularly maintained by means of auditors employed on the registrant's own staff. The accountant shall review the accounting procedures followed by the person or persons whose statements are certified and by appropriate measures shall satisfy himself that such accounting procedures are in fact being followed."[19]

In the second place the Commission has required that audits shall be as inclusive as "independent accountants would ordinarily employ." Although there could easily be difference of opinion in some instances as to whether any procedure is customarily employed, the authority of the Commision to speak decisively is not to be questioned, for it has power to prescribe the "methods to be followed in the preparation of accounts."[20]

Principles of Accounting

A recent release of the Commission states:

"If any significant change in accounting principle or practice,

---

[19]S.E.C., Securities Act Release No. 2460, February 5, 1941,
[20]Securities Act Section 19(a),

or any significant retroactive adjustment of the accounts of prior years, has been made at the beginning of or during any period covered by the profit and loss statements filed, a statement thereof shall be given in a note to the appropriate statement, and, if the change or adjustment substantially affects proper comparison with the preceding fiscal period, the necessary explanation.''[21]

The attitude of the Commission toward principles of accounting to be employed is illustrated in the case of the Monroe Loan Society.[22] Discovery of the unsatisfactory principle used might never have occurred had it not been that the registrant, some months after its statement became effective, notified the Commission of a series of defalcations by the manager of one of its offices. In stop order proceedings[23] the Commission learned that the independent accountants had not made an examination of branch office accounts even though the certificate stated that the ''examination in respect to the branch office records was sufficient in scope to satisfy ourselves as to the correctness of those accounts.''[24] At no time during the entire life of the company throughout the ten-year period prior to November 30, 1937, had independent accountants visited any branch office to examine notes, records of loans, or assets. Employing its policy of allowing certified public accountants to ''give due weight to an internal system of audit regularly maintained'' by a registrant, the Commission concluded that accountants for this company had completely disregarded customary procedure in the accounting profession for keeping the records of farm loan companies.

---

[21]S.E.C., Securities Act Release No. 2460, February 5, 1941.

[22]III Decisions 407.

[23]No stop order was issued inasmuch as amendments corrected the deficiencies.

[24]III Decisions, p. 410. Another illustration of the carelessness of accountants may be found in the opinion of the Commission in the Illinois Zinc Company Case, VI Decisions 850.

CHAPTER IX

THE NEW CONTROLS

The controls which have been established for the protection of investors are to be adjudged on the basis of their effectiveness in eliminating opportunities for exploitation, for the Securities Act was directed against the exploiter and the exploiter alone. To appraise the success of the Act and its administration it is necessary, therefore, to determine what limitations, if any, have been imposed upon those who might wish to make use of the practices delineated in the opening chapter of this study.

COMMON STOCKHOLDERS

The promoter has almost as great legal freedom as ever to obtain excessive rewards for his services. The Commission has found fault in at least one case,[1] with the amount of the promoter's pay, but even though it may entertain an opinion that a promoter is about to profit more than he deserves, that in itself could hardly justify a stop order. So long as there is complete disclosure as to what the promoter is to be paid (assuming that no law other than the Securities Act is violated), there is no way for the Commission to interfere.[2] It may be, however, that the mere fact of

---

[1]*Brandy-Wine Brewing Company*, I Decisions 136.

[2]If, as in the Brandy-Wine case, the law of the state in which the issuer is domiciled requires that promoters be compensated on the basis of past services, the Commission can, presumably, issue a stop order if promoters' services have been grossly overvalued.

disclosure promotes restraint. It was the belief of those who devised the Securities Act that publicity would be a preventive of abuse, but sweeping conclusions as to the effectiveness of publicity as a weapon of social control cannot be made with assurance, particularly insofar as it relates to control over security issuance, for there are great diversities in the motives which lead people to buy securities. There is often so much uncertainty as to how an investment will turn out that many persons are willing to disregard the facts which are made available to them and invest their money in the hope that profits will be commensurate with the risk. Former Chairman Joseph P. Kennedy has declared that the Commission "actually warned scores of men and women on an amazing sucker list that they were in danger of being swindled, yet with this official warning many of them trotted out calmly to be sheared, actually buying securities from the dubious concern they were warned against."[3]

Officers and other employees, as well as underwriters, are, like promoters, under no direct federal control with respect to the amounts or kinds of rewards they receive for their services. Except insofar as the opinions of actual or prospective investors may exercise a restraining influence upon boards of directors in fixing terms of compensation, the opportunity for exploiting stockholders by paying certain persons excessive prices for their services is as great as ever.

The Purchase of Property at Excessive Prices

It is not so simple as it once was for corporations to buy the property of favorites at abnormally high prices. The

[3]*Saturday Evening Post*, January 18, 1936.

Commission exercises no control over managerial discretion with reference to prices that are actually paid, but complete disclosure is required. It may seem inconsistent to say that all the law requires is complete disclosure of promoters' rewards and of prices that are paid for property, but that although the promoter is at no disadvantage in the sale of his services except insofar as the fear of publicity acts as a restraining influence, the opportunity for paying excessive prices for property has been reduced. The apparent inconsistency is to be explained by the fact that the problem of valuing the services of promoters is quite different from the problem of valuing property—particularly physical property. The Commission has not yet been bold enough to suggest standards for valuing the services of promoters. If a promoter (or any other person rendering service to a corporation) were to be paid for routine activities, it might be easy enough to make an estimate of what his contributions were worth, but it is difficult, if not impossible, to evaluate those intangible qualities of service which spring from the imagination and which find expression in ability to organize, to inspire, or to execute plans daringly.

The Commission appears to be much more certain of its ground when it deals with valuations of property. If value is based upon cost, and cost was high merely because of the bad judgment of those who were responsible for buying, the Commission is not interested; but if cost was high and the buyer had direct or indirect affiliations with the seller, overvaluation may be regarded as false or misleading. When value is the result of an appraisal, the representations of the registrant may be attacked if the principles of appraisal or their application are regarded by the Commission as unacceptable.

It is when stock is to be issued for property that the temptation to be generous is most pronounced. This may be due to a desire to pay the promoter or someone in the employ of the corporation for property and services without giving any recognition in the accounts to the fact that services had been rendered. In other cases it may be the result of a desire to circumscribe the law requiring the sale of stock at no less than par, by issuing excessive amounts of it for property with the understanding that portions are to be returned as a gift to be sold subsequently for any price the corporation can get for it. Although it was once customary for corporations to issue excessive amounts of stock in exchange for property, the Securities Act has made such procedure much more difficult. The Commission will not allow the pay of promoters to be charged to the property account, and if it finds that property has been overvalued, it will require that the valuation be modified.

The Sale of Stock at Varying Prices[4]

The sale of stock at varying prices can endanger the position of common stockholders only when they are kept in ignorance of facts which they ought to know in order to appraise opportunities for purchasing new issues or when they are denied the preemptive right. The Securities Act has improved the position of stockholders seeking greater light upon the experiences of their corporations, but the status of the preemptive right remains unchanged. It is still possible for an issuer to grant options or to limit its sales of securities to a selected group. If there is complete disclosure of its intentions, there is no way for the Commission to interfere with plans to extend to insiders the exclu-

---

[4]See Note 9 of Chapter I.

sive privilege of subscribing to new stock, provided the issuer has a right under its charter to make such a limitation.

The registration statement may be helpful, however, to stockholders who are not invited to participate in the purchase of the new issue. It may possibly contain information which can be used in supporting a suit charging that the subscription price was fixed at an inequitably low level. If those who do not have subscription rights are able to show that the price to those who bought was inequitably low, the corporation can then recover the difference between the price at which purchases were made and the price at which the stock should have been sold, in the judgment of the court, in order to prevent the transfer of equities from those who did not subscribe to those who actually bought.

The Sale of Assets at Low Prices to Purchasers With Whom the Issuers are Affiliated

A corporation which wishes to sell substantial portions of its assets for cash (or the securities of a purchasing corporation), can do so without being affected by the Securities Act. This is true whether small amounts of property are sold from time to time or large amounts are sold at particular moments. The purchaser may have cash which it has accumulated from operations or it may have to sell securities in order to get cash with which to make payment. If the sale of new securities is subject to the Securities Act, it will have to file a registration statement in which its plans for the purchase will need to be set forth. So far as the published record discloses, the Commission has never had an interest in whether the security holders of a corporation which sells property are exploited; nor has it been interested in preventing a registrant from getting a bargain when it plans to buy property. The Securities Act affords outside stockholders no protection against the sale of assets at low prices when the sale is for cash. The only hope of minorities in such instances is that they may attain the unlikely objective of convincing courts that they ought to deal more realistically with the problem of valuation than courts have characteristically done in the past.

Nor has the position of the minority stockholder been improved, necessarily, by the Securities Act, when sales of assets take the form of mergers or consolidations which terminate the existence of corporations in which the minorities are interested. There are two classes of mergers in which the Securities and Exchange Commission is *not* interested. The Act itself extends exemption to securities which are issued in exchange for the securities of other organizations when the program for exchange has been approved by a court, or other public agency authorized to test its fairness, after any of those whose interests are to be affected have had opportunity to present their opinions with respect to the plan of exchange.[5]

The Commission has extended exemption to securities issued in connection with mergers and consolidations, provided stockholders approve the change by "vote of the required favorable majority" and provided their action will "authorize the transfer or ... effectuate the merger or consolidation" and "will bind all stockholders" of the corporation except those electing to exercise their right of appraisal.[6]

It is conceivable that protection of minorities may be

---

[5]Section 3(10), as amended in 1934. See Section 202 of the Act of 1934. If bonds are issued, the indenture must qualify under the Act of 1939.
[6]Rule 5(3) for Form E-1.

ample when mergers or consolidations occur under judicial scrutiny, but it is impossible to say as much in behalf of mergers or consolidations which occur in conformity with statutory requirements.[7] The ease with which exploitation may occur is illustrated in the following hypothetical case: Corporation A proposes to absorb Corporation B. Each is capitalized at $100,000. For the sake of simplifying the illustration it will be assumed that the property of each is valued in the records at $100,000. The property of A is really worth $95,000 and the property of B is really worth $105,000. X owns all the stock of A and half the stock of B. The plan which A has for the absorption of B is approved in the statutory manner, and A issues one share of stock for each share that B has had outstanding. If after the merger occurs, A were to sell all its property for $200,000 and distribute the cash as a liquidating dividend, X would receive as his share the sum of $150,000. Had there been no merger and had each of the two companies dissolved under circumstances enabling them to get $95,000 and $105,000 respectively for their property, the share of X would have been $147,500.

It should be added that registration under the Securities Act of the securities issued by A for the outstanding securities of B would not necessarily have prevented the transfer of equity from the outside stockholders of B to X, but if the Commission had made thoroughgoing inquiry into the al-

---

[7] "The usual steps in statutory consolidation or merger include the following: (1) An agreement as to terms, often drawn up by the directors or a committee and issued to the shareholders of the corporations to be consolidated into a new corporation. (2) Submission of the agreement to the stockholders of each company at a meeting thereof. (3) Acceptance of the agreement by a majority vote, or by a two-thirds or three-quarters vote if required. (4) Filing of the articles or agreement of consolidation in the office of the secretary of state, as in the case of a new incorporation and payments of fees." Ballantine, *Private Corporations*, p. 753.

leged valuation of the property of both *A* and *B* and had insisted upon modification of the value of each, the outside stockholders of *B* would have had a better basis than they presumably had for deciding whether the merger ought to have been effected. If the Commission should choose to modify its policy with respect to such situations, it is conceivable that the Securities Act might come to have some significance to minority stockholders of corporations about to enter mergers or consolidations.

Speculation in Securities on the Basis of Inside Information

The freedom of issuers to determine what items of information required in reports to the Commission shall continue to have the status of secrecy has been greatly circumscribed. The Securities Act gives the Commission power to withhold the publication of material contracts if publicity "would impair the value of the contract and would not be necessary for the protection of investors."[8] It is to ancillary legislation, however, that the investor must look for any protection afforded by law, against loss arising from speculation by insiders on the basis of their knowledge of business secrets.

The legislation of 1934 requires a report by the tenth of each month from every officer or principal stockholder of any organization with securities listed on national securi-

---

[8]Item 30, Schedule A. See also Rule 580 of General Rules and Regulations under the Securities Act. The Securities Exchange Act (Section 24) likewise gives the Commission power to publish items which issuers would like to have given the status of secrecy. During the fiscal year of 1938 twenty-one Securities Act registrants filed requests that information regarding material contracts be given a confidential status. Seventeen of the requests were granted, in whole or in part. During the same year approval was given to sixty-one of the one hundred and thirty-nine applications of a similar kind filed under the Securities Exchange Act. S.E.C., *Fourth Annual Report*, p. 731.

ties exchanges,[9] whose ownership of any class of equity security has undergone a change during the preceding month. The data which are thus accumulated are summarized by the Commission and published in the form of releases which are available without cost to any person who may wish to obtain them.

Stock market commentators have long emphasized the fact that substantial changes in business are often anticipated by weeks or months by changes in the movements of the stock averages. This, they have explained, has occurred at least in part because of the speculative activities of insiders who had knowledge of what the prospects of their organizations were and traded on that knowledge to their own personal advantage. It may appear that the benefits of inside knowledge can be transferred to outside stockholders of a corporation by requiring the insiders to make available to the public in general such intimations of their judgments of corporate outlook as may be suggested by changes which take place in their ownership of its securities. Whether this is a valid assumption is open to question, for changes in outlook often occur very quickly and modifications in the investments of insiders may take place long before outside investors can be apprised of what has happened. When the reports of the Commission are ready for publication, some of the most recent transactions included occurred several weeks earlier. Persons who are not greatly concerned about fluctuations in the market value of securities but are interested in long time investment are not likely to give attention to reports of insiders' transactions. At the other extreme is the short term speculator who may be

[9] A principal stockholder, as that expression is used here, being one who has a direct or indirect interest in any class of equity securities which amounts to as much as 10% of the issue. Securities Exchange Act, Section 16.

in and out of a security several times during a period of from one to two months.   Changes in the ownership of securities are meaningless, moreover, without knowledge of the circumstances which led to the changes.   Speculative advantages constitute but one of many possible reasons for buying or selling.

The judgment of a corporate officer as to the prospects for his organization is not, moreover, to be determined by how much of its stock he owns at any time.   He may not be interested in investment or speculation, and even if he is, he may find that the securities of other corporations are much more attractive.   The securities which interest him may have been issued by organizations in other industries or they may have been issued by competitive corporations engaged in the same industry of which his own is a part. If he knows the prospects for the corporation with which he is identified, he presumably knows the prospects for competitive organizations.   He can buy and sell their securities without having to make reports to the Securities and Exchange Commission so long as he does not become an officer or principal stockholder in any one of them.   If he resents publicity regarding changes in his ownership of securities, he can avoid it by speculating in the securities of enterprises with which he is not affiliated as an officer or principal stockholder.[10]

The legislation of 1934 provides a second weapon for use

---

[10]The advice of insiders may be very helpful, too, to their own families, for the General Counsel of the Commission has expressed the opinion that the ''mere fact that a wife, as a bookkeeping matter, keeps the securities in her separate estate is not conclusive in determining whether her husband is the beneficial owner. . . . Whether or not the husband is the beneficial owner of such securities depends upon whether by reason of any contract, understanding, relationship, agreement or other arrangement, he has benefits substantially equivalent to those of ownership.'' S.E.C., Securities Exchange Act Release No. 175, April 16, 1935,

against the insider who speculates on the basis of information not generally available. Any officer, director, or principal stockholder of an organization whose securities are listed on national securities exchanges may be deprived of profits which he makes out of transactions in its securities provided he owned them less than six months.[11] The law specifies, however, not that the person who profits shall pay voluntarily but that the profits shall "inure to and be recoverable by the issuer"; and that if the issuer, which might be under the domination of the officer, director, or principal stockholder involved, does not choose to take appropriate action, any security holder may sue "in the name and in behalf of the issuer."

Knowledge of accounting policies with respect to such matters as depreciation and obsolescence is of vital significance to the speculator. If depreciation charges have not been adequate, the registrant may get into trouble with the Commission. It is the duty of the independent accountant who examines financial statements to pass judgment upon accounting procedures and their use by the registrant. If he approves a depreciation policy which does not provide for adequate depreciation charges, the Commission may focus public attention upon his untrustworthiness as an accountant. Overvaluation of property is probably much more common than undervaluation. Although the Commission expects seasoned registrants which have made significant revaluations of property since 1922 to provide information about all such transactions,[12] whether the revaluations have been up or down, there is no published evidence that it has ever been concerned about secret re-

---

[11]Section 16(b). He is exempt from this provision if the securities which were sold at a profit were "acquired in good faith in connection with a debt previously contracted."
[12]Item 45, Form A-2.

serves which may have arisen as a consequence of generous depreciation charges. If depreciation charges are excessive, it is the responsibility of the independent accountant to say so. It is very easy, however, to justify generous charges on the ground that such a policy evidences conservatism in financial management.

There are no ways of knowing to what extent registrants have developed secret reserves of which the Commission is uninformed, nor is there any way of knowing whether the Commission has been concerned about such reserves if it knew of their existence. If it is to assume responsibility, as it has done, for requiring downward revisions of items of value which it believes to be overstated, it is difficult to see how it could justify failure to require that the veil of secrecy be lifted from all reserves. The buyer of securities who does not already have an investment in the issuer will not be injured by any secret reserves that exist at the time of his purchase. If the preemptive right prevails, however, and new stock is to be sold, those stockholders who have complete confidence in the integrity of published financial statements and who are therefore uninformed of the existence of a secret reserve, may refuse to buy and may sell their stock rights for less than they are worth. The stockholder, moreover, who parts with his stock without knowing that his corporation has certain items of value of which it tells him nothing may for that reason be just as effectively exploited as though he had bought stock in another corporation without knowing that property values had been exaggerated.

Modifications of Claims to Assets and Income

Modifications of claims to assets and income by formal action of a board of directors occur only when stock has been classified. The Securities Act has done nothing to restrict opportunities for such modifications except to require information from registrants upon such matters as dividend rights (including limitations upon payments of dividends), voting rights, liquidating rights, redemption provisions, and liability for further calls.[13] To the extent that information about these items may generate in investors a spirit of caution, the Act will have restricted the opportunity of boards of directors to shift claims to assets and income from one group to another within the corporation. The New York Stock Exchange, by refusing to admit to its list new issues of classified common, has probably done more than the Government to discourage the emergence of fresh opportunities for the exploitation of one class of common stockholders by another.

PREFERRED STOCKHOLDERS

The Securities Act has provided no protection to preferred stockholders who may be virtually forced to surrender their stock and their claims to accumulated dividends in exchange for other securities. An issuer planning to trade new prior preferred for outstanding preferred does not have to register the new issue if it is to be offered to none but its own security holders and "no commission or other remuneration is paid or given directly or indirectly for soliciting such exchange."[14] Even though registration of the new issue might occur, there is no authority for the Commission to consider the fairness of the proposed plan of reorganization. So far as the Securities Act is concerned, the status of the preferred stockholder remains unchanged

[13] See Item 16, Form A-2.
[14] Section 3(a)9.

when he is asked to accept a new issue for the claims he already has.

The Commission has made use of one provision in the Securities Exchange Act, however,[15] in an effort to render assistance to the helpless preferred stockholder. It has authority under that Act to regulate the solicitations of proxies for securities which are listed on national securities exchanges. There is no control over proxies if preferred stock is not listed on such an exchange or if the owner does not have a right to an expression of opinion through the use of the voting privilege when the corporation considers adding an amendment to its charter authorizing the issuance of prior preferred.

Even when proxies are solicited, the Commission can require nothing more than publicity with regard to certain past experiences of the issuer, the plans which it has for the immediate future and the interests of those who engage in solicitation.[16] If the solicitors comply with the wishes of the Commission in furnishing stockholders with information by which they may be guided in their responses to proxy solicitations, they may proceed without interference.

That the authority of the Commission to regulate proxy solicitations has had great significance in protecting preferred stockholders is to be doubted. The Commission found fault in 1936 with information filed by one company which was interested in soliciting proxies in preparation for modification of the position of its preferred stockholders. It asked the organization to recircularize its "stockholders with supplemental information which would correct any

---

[15]Section 14.

[16]For a statement of the information required in such cases see especially Item 10, Rule X-14-A-1. See also S.E.C., Securities Exchange Act Release No. 2376, January 12, 1940. Rule X-14A-2 gives stockholders a right to determine how their proxies shall be exercised in some cases.

misimpression that the stockholders might have formed from the original material.'"[17] When the company refused to comply with this request, the Commission released a statement of its own in which it called attention to facts that it believed the stockholders ought to have. The statement did not have great influence, however, for the plan was approved at the stockholders' meeting which occurred shortly after the release was issued.[18]

It is important that preferred stockholders have access to information regarding the implications of plans of reorganization which they may be asked to approve. It is nearly always inevitable that some stockholders will grant proxies without examining the information which is available or without being influenced by it. Still others may understand the implications and realize the futility of trying to interfere with the proposed reorganization. When the issuer holds out a promise of immediate and regular dividends to owners of the new prior preferred and suggests that resumption of dividends on the old preferred can be expected, if at all, only at some unpredictable time in the future, the holder of preferred needs something besides information if he is to resist the temptation to accept the proposed offer of settlement. What protection society can afford the preferred stockholder is not apparent. It might seem that he would have a guarantee of adequate protection if plans of reorganization with potentiality for imperilling his interest could be declared effective only after approval of a court or other public agency. Bondholders generally have such protection, but there is no certainty that it would

---

[17]*Report on Protective and Reorganization Committees*, Part VII, p. 141.

[18]The plan was later set aside, however, by the Delaware Court of Chancery on the ground that a Delaware corporation could not force preferred stockholders, by mere charter amendment, to accept modification of their claims to dividends.

have significance to preferred shareholders. Whereas bond-holders as creditors have enforceable claims, preferred stockholders as owners are in a weak bargaining position. They cannot demand payment of accumulated dividends. The solvency of a corporation is in no way imperilled because it is behind in dividend payments to preferred stock-holders. If plans of reorganization were subject to judicial approval, and if preferred stockholders refused to accept a proposed plan but suggested one of their own which the corporation rejected, the result might well be maintenance of the status quo. The corporation might be even more determined than ever to continue the policy of refusing to pay preferred stockholders any dividends. There might be instances, on the other hand, in which judicial review would result in compromises that might be to the advantage of the preferred stockholder.

BONDHOLDERS

The position of the bondholder has been considerably improved as a result of two recent laws: The modification of the bankruptcy law in 1938 and the Trust Indenture Act of 1939. The specific modification of the Bankruptcy Act in 1938 which has great potentiality for promoting the welfare of bondholders in reorganizations is that provision which requires courts of bankruptcy to submit proposed plans of reorganization to the Securities and Exchange Commission for investigation and report if the total debt of the organization is in excess of three million dollars, and which permits the court to turn to the Commission for assistance in other cases.[19] The Commission is under no obliga-

---

[19]See Section 171 to 179, inclusive, of Public Number 696, 75th Congress, 3rd Session.

tion to report upon any plan of reorganization but if it chooses to do so, its opinion or a summary which meets with its approval must be sent by the trustee to all "creditors and stockholders who are affected by any such plan." Dispassionate, unbiased, and authoritative discussions of plans of reorganization can be of incalculable value to security holders if such discussions are made available to them prior to the time when they must either accept or reject the work of a reorganization committee.

The Securities and Exchange Commission has no power, it should be added, to impose its will with respect to any reorganization. It can act only in an advisory capacity, but if it chooses to make a report, its opinions must be made available to those who are able to give or withhold approval of proposed plans of reorganization. The value of such opinions depends upon the general level of skill of the Commission in dealing with the issues which are presented by the Bankruptcy Act and the exhaustiveness of the work which it does in individual cases.

As a matter of practice it always undertakes to obtain all 'he information it can get about the affairs of any corpora-'ion in whose reorganization it is to share. Its own attorneys and analysts are available for such services as they are able to render to those who formulate plans of reorganization. The Commission is ready to aid trustees in the discharge of their duties. Sometimes trustees are given instruction with regard to their responsibilities and how they may be discharged most successfully. The Commission always insists that trustees prepare and submit to security holders reports upon "the property, liabilities, and financial condition of the debtor, the operation of its business and the desirability of the continuance thereof."[20] Many

---
[20]Section 167(5).

costs are subject to the criticism of the Commission. Its extensive experience with certain experts—notably accountants—has provided it with an excellent basis of judgment as to the value of their services. It is also interested in seeing that "unnecessary duplication of services shall not be recompensed."[21] More important, probably, than any of its work under the Bankruptcy Act, is its study of the feasibility and fairness of proposed plans of reorganization.

"The Commission has consistently taken the position that the applicable standard of fairness in reorganization proceedings requires that a plan, to be fair, must provide fully compensatory treatment for claims in the order of their legal and contractual priority, either in cash or new securities or both, and that the participation granted to junior claims must be based either upon the existence of an equity for them in the enterprise after the satisfaction of prior claims or upon a fresh contribution in money or money's worth necessary to the reorganization of the debtor. A valuation of the debtor is necessary to provide the basis for judging the fairness and feasibility of proposed plans of reorganization. In its advisory reports, in hearings before courts, and in conferences with parties to proceedings, the Commission has consistently taken the position that the proper method of valuation for reorganization purposes is primarily the capitalization of reasonably prospective earnings."[22]

New Position of Trustees and Reorganization Committees

The prospective bondholder, if the issue in which he is interested is subject to the act of 1939, may now have assurance that the trustee has adequate financial responsibility; that the issuer records mortgages; that the proceeds of the sale of bonds are applied to the purposes advertised in the prospectus; that substitutions of security for the issue will occur, if at all, only after there has been a satisfactory ap-

---

[21]S.E.C., *Sixth Annual Report*, p. 62.
[22]*Ibid.*, 65.

praisal of the property to be released from the lien and assurance from a competent expert that the release "will not impair the security under such indenture"; that property which is to be used as the basis of an increase in the amount of outstanding bonds has been fairly valued; that default will be announced promptly unless delay is authorized in the manner provided in the law; that the trustee will not be allowed to continue indefinitely in a conflicting position; and that it will not be permitted to get an unfair advantage when it undertakes to salvage its own investments in the issuer in violation of its pledge to bondholders. Reorganization committees are as free as ever to make ironclad deposit agreements with bondholders, but the Trust Indenture Act has deprived them of a powerful weapon in its provisions relative to lists of bondholders' names. To the bonds outstanding in 1939, however, the new law does not apply.

THE DANGERS OF THE PRESENT POLICY

If the registration statement may be regarded as the foundation, the prospectus is the cornerstone of present federal policy in the regulation of securities distribution. It is the prospectus and the prospectus alone that can be of immediate significance to the average investor. With the authority that it has, the Commission can be almost as inquisitive as it likes about the experiences of registrants. Statements may accordingly be about as voluminous as the Commission chooses to make them, but if the information which is accumulated is to be of value it must be made available to those who wish to use it. If the Commission is to do more for investors than prevent the sale of certain securities and provide a repository of information which may be

useful to lawyers in supporting suits for rescission of sale
and damages, it ought to promote the distribution among
investors of useful and usable facts about registrants. The
assumption of the Securities Act is that a great many people are willing to be rational about investment policies
whenever they have adequate factual information which
they can use in making investment decisions.

The Investor May Be Confused

In controlling the content of prospectuses the Commission has been anxious to provide investors with a great deal
of information and has required the inclusion of such a
great volume of data that many investors have been over-
whelmed. Perhaps they ought to know much more about
investment analysis than they do and to be anxious for all
the facts they can get. At the present time, however, the
prolixity of certain prospectuses is very confusing.

The investor may likewise be confused as to the purpose
of the Securities Act. Try as it may to persuade investors
that its examinations of registration statements are not
equivalent to a guarantee, the Securities and Exchange
Commission cannot possibly convince them that its examination of statements is no assurance of investment merit.
Those who know a great deal about the Securities Act and
its administration and are therefore familiar with the meticulous care the Commission uses in studying statements
during the waiting period are tempted to feel a measure of
confidence in securities whose registration statements have
become completely effective merely because the statements
have been subjected to critical examination by the Commission.

In the sense that investors have been denied the right to buy issues which, purely because of the Act, have not been sold, there has been modification of investment opportunity. This has been good to the extent that such opportunities might have resulted in loss to investors. It is possible, however, that the Securities Act has been a discouragement to many organizations—particularly small organizations—which without the Act would have issued securities with investment merit, but which because of the Act have been restrained from doing so. Private selling of securities has deprived numerous investors of opportunities to purchase securities of high quality. Although it is to be regretted that corporations which might issue first class securities are discouraged from doing so and that our existing policy regarding private sales gives institutional investors an advantage which was not anticipated when the law was passed in 1933, modifications of investment opportunity which have taken place as a consequence of these developments have invariably occurred without doing violence to the spirit of the law.

There is another modification which can be made, very quietly, under the leadership of Commissioners committed to an entirely different policy from that which Congress intended to establish when it passed the Securities Act; that is, modification which is based upon the policy of regulating the flow of capital into industry. Commenting upon the administration of the Act, former Chairman James M. Landis has said,

"The major reforms in regard to underwriting practice, corporate disclosure, and accounting techniques that the Commission has brought about—and it has brought about many—are not of public record. The trend of decisional policy is not readily discoverable from the stop order opinions of the Commission. The nature of these reforms can only be found by an examination of the successive amendments made by issuers of securities prior to the effective date—amendments made in the hope that the corrected form of disclosure will avert the bringing of a proceeding.''[23]

A democratic society is in a potentially dangerous situation when the policies of an administrative agency which has far-reaching power to regulate capital markets can be known only by those who are on the inside. The danger is so much the greater when the agency deals, in a confidential manner, with each registrant separately and there is no way for any one of them to know how the demands that are made upon it compare with the demands made upon others except insofar as the others may publicize these demands or insofar as an examination of amendments to registration statements may provide basis for inferences.

Registrants have protection, it is alleged, because of the right which the Act gives them to appeal from decisions of the Commission. It is easy to exaggerate the practical significance of this right. The market for capital is never static. Timing of security distributions is of basic importance. A delay of but a few days may prevent the sale of an issue which could readily have been sold under earlier circumstances. An issuer is therefore more likely than not to be in a necessitous condition when it receives a deficiency letter from the Commission. Whatever its judgment as to the wisdom or legal necessity of the demand that has been made upon it, it will ordinarily be disposed to forget about its rights and comply, if that is possible, rather than run the risk of having the condition of the capital market change in such a way as to prevent successful distribution of its issue.

---

[23] James M. Landis, *The Administrative Process,* p. 109, New Haven (1938).

A registrant has no right, moreover, to appeal from opinions which are expressed in a deficiency letter. The deficiency letter is not an order; it is merely an expression of opinion of one of the divisions of the Commission that the registration statement is deficient. Until the Commission issues an order denying effectiveness to the statement, there is nothing the registrant can do about asking for judicial review of its case. And before a stop order is issued, there must be a hearing and a trial before the Commission. A reputable corporation which is asked to make modifications in its statement that it regards as unreasonable and inconsistent with the purposes of the Act may choose to withdraw its statement and forego the sale of its securities rather than submit to the humiliation of a public trial and a possible stop order.

Organizations May Be Handicapped in Getting Capital

Capricious administration of the law[24] might easily result in unwillingness of organizations to prepare statements or in the withdrawal of statements, already on file, which had not become effective. There is no way of knowing whether this factor may have prevented any issue from being sold. The financial burden, which compliance with the Act entails, has been a genuine handicap to many organizations, but here again, there is no way of knowing how significant the factor of cost has been in preventing the flotation of new securities. It is hardly to be doubted that many small organizations have found the Act a very substantial handicap.

The issuer of small amounts of securities has two different kinds of disadvantages. The costs incident to registration are relatively much heavier than those which must be

---

[24] *Annalist*, July 13, 1939, p. 36.

met when the issue is large;[25] and there is no immediate escape from the burden, as there may be for the larger issuer, for institutional investors are less interested in small issues than in large ones. The ultimate incidence of these costs may sometimes be such, however, as to give the issuer no concern. The requirements of registration may cause some issuers to make a reexamination of certain problems of management. If there have been wastes which are brought to their attention for the first time because of the advice of outside experts who are employed to assist in the preparation of registration statements, reorganization may reduce the wastes at least enough to pay the cost of registration. An example would be improvement in utilization of machinery which would increase the length of its life. The reorganization might, however, result in such an improvement in the quality of labor that the burden would have to be borne by certain laborers with whose services the issuer could dispense or by those who might be required to work under increased tension. The burden may sometimes be shifted backward. If the process of reorganization might result in such improvement in the processing of materials, for example, that less would be wasted, those supplying these materials would bear the burden of registration costs.

In other cases investors may pay. Insofar as investors have greater confidence in securities, merely because registration statements for them are in effect, they are willing to pay all or a part of registration expenses. If, moreover, one assumes no decline in the demand for securities com-

---

[25]In May, 1940, the Commission published a study entitled *Cost of Flotation for Small Issues, 1925-1929 and 1935-1938*. As between the two periods, the cost of floating small bond issues declined from 6% to 4.8% of proceeds. The cost of flotation of small issues of preferred stock increased from 7.8% in 1925-1929 to 10.2% in 1935-1938.

mensurate with limitations on the supply for which the Securities Act is responsible, the resulting increase in price
over prices that would otherwise have prevailed will assist
the issuer in paying the cost of registration, perhaps even
relieve it of the entire burden.

In other cases the underwriter may have to bear all or a
part of the cost. A smaller volume of business since 1933
may have promoted a keener competitive spirit in the investment banking industry. The interest of the Commission in focusing attention upon spreads and in publicizing
any direct or indirect community of interest between the
issuer and the banker may possibly have contributed to the
development of that competitive spirit. Declines in banking spreads are not to be regarded, however, as prima facie
evidence that investment banking is less profitable than it
would be without the Securities Act, all other things being
the same. Some bankers may have discovered new ways of
economizing, or smaller spreads may be due to nothing
more than the reallocation of responsibility for gathering
information about the issuer.

The consumer may be adversely affected in some cases.
In such instances the issuer will sell new securities only if
the consumer is prepared to pay all the costs of registration
that cannot otherwise be shifted. If the cost of registration
is determinative in a company's decision about a projected
security issue, and if the decision is to offer no securities
for sale because of fear that competitive relationships will
be disturbed, the consumer may be worse off than he would
have been without the Securities Act. What the results in
any such case will be must depend upon what would have
happened had the securities actually been issued. If increase in the supply of capital of one competitor had initiated a cycle of price cutting, the consumer, so long as the

lower level of prices continued, would have been better off. In all such cases the Securities Act is a disadvantage, at least temporarily, to consumers.

In other cases the incidence of the cost of registration may be upon the issuer, to be borne in some instances by the common stockholders and in others by preferred stockholders or even bondholders. Illustrative of the latter would be the case of a corporation which has income bonds outstanding and which issues common stock, proceeds from which are so unwisely invested that the corporation earns less than it would have earned had the stock never been sold. If the earnings which are available to pay interest upon income bonds are for that reason less than enough to pay the full amount, a part of the cost of getting the new capital and hence, presumably, a part of the cost of registration will have been shifted to income bondholders.

There are certain circumstances under which it may be impossible for an issuer to shift the burden. This may be true if it happens to be in a necessitous condition arising from the fact that it has a maturing bond issue which must be refunded, or that it is under obligation to meet some urgent public requirement such as making immediate provision for elimination of a smoke nuisance, or that it is unable to renew its short term notes and must have long time capital to take care of its constant working capital needs. In these and other cases like them the issuer may find that shifting the cost of registration is impossible.

The amount of new capital which corporations have secured through the sale of securities since 1933 has been quite inconsiderable. The Securities Act has been partly to blame for this fact, particularly in the case of small corporations which have found the requirements of registration peculiarly onerous. There are other circumstances, however, which have been considerably more important than the Securities Act in the decisions of corporations not to seek fresh outside capital. Since 1933 there has been no new industry which required such amounts of capital as went into the motor industry after the close of the first World War. Many corporations, moreover, have ceased to be dependent upon the help of outside capitalists.

"A significant characteristic of a highly developed industrial system is the increasing importance of depreciation and depletion allowances as a source of funds for capital outlays on renewal and replacement of plant and equipment. When a society has accumulated a vast stock of capital goods, it is evident that the mere expenditure of depreciation allowances provides wide scope for continuous improvement of plant and equipment. . . . Obviously a society with large depreciation and depletion allowances can modernize and improve its capital equipment, introducing continually new techniques, and even at times expanding its plant and equipment without tapping any new savings."[26]

The government has, besides, undertaken new activities, some of which under earlier circumstances would have been privately financed. Taxes and sales of government bonds tap income and savings, at least some of which might otherwise have been used for the purchase of corporate securities. According to Professor Pigou and Colin Clark,[27] savings in Great Britain prior to 1914 were equal to about 12% or 13% of total income, but by 1935 they amounted to no more than 7%. In the meantime, however, the proportion of total national income spent by the government for social services had increased from about 3% just before the war to about 12% in 1935.[28]

---

[26]Statement of testimony of Professor A. H. Hansen before the Temporary National Economic Committee Hearing, T.N.E.C., 76th Congress, 1st Session, Part 9, p. 3538.
[27]*Economic Position of Great Britain.*
[28]Hansen, *op. cit.*, p. 16.

Unless the government is to assume responsibility for directing the flow of capital into industry, there are limits to what it ought to do for investors. It cannot safely act as their guardians; it cannot afford to become a bulwark of defense against all the hazards which exist in the securities markets. In a society like ours, it should regard itself as a sentry assigned to hold back the exploiter and warn the army of investors of his presence whenever he breaks through the outer defenses.

BIBLIOGRAPHY

Ashby, Forest Bee, *The Economic Effect of Blue Sky Laws*, Philadelphia, 1926.

Attorney General's Committee on Administrative Procedure: *The Securities and Exchange Commission*, Washington.

Ballantine, Arthur, "Amending the Securities Act," *American Bar Association Journal*, 20: 85 (1934).

Bane, Baldwin, "Federal Securities Act of 1933," *Boston University Law Review*, 14: 35 (1933).

Barnett, George E., "The Securities Act of 1933 and the British Companies Act," *Harvard Business Review*, 13: 1 (1934).

Bates, George E., "Some Effects of the Securities Act upon Investment Banking Practices," *Law and Contemporary Problems*, IV: 72 (1937).

Bates, George E., "The Waiting Period under the Securities Act," *Harvard Business Review*, 15: 203 (1937).

Berle, A. A., and Means, Gardiner, *The Modern Corporation and Private Property*, New York, 1933.

Berle, A. A., "High Finance: Master or Servant," *Yale Review*, 23: 20 (1933).

Blough, Carman, "The Relationship of the Securities and Exchange Commission to the Accountant," *Journal of Accountancy*, 63: 23 (1937).

Brandeis, Louis, *Other People's Money*, New York, 1913.

Burtchett, F. F., *Corporation Finance*, New York, 1934.

Cale, Edward G., "A Study of Ineffective Investment Trust and Precious Metal Mining Issues," *Law and Contemporary Problems*, IV: 32 (1937).

Congressional Publications: H. R. 12603, 66th Congress, 2nd Session; H. R. 188, 66th Congress, 1st Session; H. R. 7215, 67th Congress, 1st Session; H. R. 10598, 67th Congress, 4th Session; H. R. 4, 68th Congress, 1st Session; H. R. 52, 69th Congress, 1st Session; H. R. 4314, 73rd Congress, 1st Session; S. 875, 73rd Congress, 1st Session; S. 2344, 75th Congress, 1st Session; H. R. 10292, 75th Congress, 3rd Session; H. R. 2191, 76th Congress, 1st Session; H. R. 5270, 76th Congress, 1st Session; House Document 1485, 65th Congress, 2nd Session; House Report 85, 73rd Congress, 1st Session; Senate Report 1455, 73rd Congress, 2nd Session.

TxU

Crane, Ralph, "Practical Effects of the Securities Act," *Journal of Accountancy*, 60: 370 (1935).

Dalton, John E., "The Development and Future Trends in State Security Regulation," *Harvard Business Review*, 12: 23 (1933).

Dean, Arthur, "Securities Act," *Fortune*, VIII: 50 (1933).

Dean, Arthur, "The Lawyer's Problems in the Registration of Securities," *Law and Contemporary Problems*, IV: 154 (1937).

Dewing, A. S., *Financial Policy of Corporations*, Fourth Revised Edition, New York (1941).

Dodd, David, *Stock Watering*, New York, 1930.

Douglas, William, "Protecting the Investor," *Yale Review*, 23: 521 (1934).

Douglas, William, and Bates, George, "The Federal Securities Act of 1933," *Yale Law Journal*, 43: 171 (1933).

Douglas, William, and Bates, George, "Some Effects of the Federal Securities Act upon Investment Banking," *Chicago Law Review*, I: 283 (1933).

Field, Kenneth, *Corporation Finance*, New York, 1938.

Flexner, Bernard, "The Fight on the Securities Act," *Atlantic Monthly*, 153: 232 (1934).

Fortas, Abe, "The Securities Act and Corporate Reorganizations," *Law and Contemporary Problems*, IV: 219 (1937).

Frankfurter, Felix, "Securities Act," *Fortune*, VIII: 53 (1933).

Gerstenberg, Charles W., *Financial Organization and Management of Business*, Second Revised Edition, New York, 1939.

Goldschmidt, R. W., "Registration under the Securities Act," *Law and Contemporary Problems*, IV: 19 (1937).

Gourrich, Paul F., "Investment Banking Methods Prior to and Since the Securities Act of 1933," *Law and Contemporary Problems*, IV: 44 (1937).

Greidinger, B. Bernard, *Accounting Requirements of the Securities and Exchange Commission for the Preparation of Financial Statements by Independent Public Accountants*, New York, 1939.

Guthmann, Harry, and Dougall, Herbert, *Corporation Financial Policy*, New York, 1940.

Hanna, John, "The Securities Exchange Act as Supplementary of the Securities Act," *Law and Contemporary Problems*, IV: 256 (1937).

Hansen, A. H., Testimony Before Temporary National Economic Committee, May 16, 1939.

Haven, T. Kenneth, *Investment Banking under the Securities and Exchange Commission*, Ann Arbor, 1940.

Hendersen, A. I. "Practice under the Securities Act of 1933 and the Securities Exchange Act of 1934 from the Viewpoint of the Attorney," *Journal of Accountancy*, 58:448 (1934).

Hoagland, Henry, *Corporation Finance*, New York, 1938.

Johnson, A. C., and Jackson, Andrew, "The Securities and Exchange Commission: Its Organization and Functions under the Securities Act," *Law and Contemporary Problems*, IV: 1 (1937).

Kessler, Friedrich, "The American Securities Act and Its Foreign Counterparts: A Comparative Study," *Yale Law Journal*, 44: 1133 (1935).

Kimball, Milo, *Corporate Finance*, New York, 1939.

Kuhn, C. John, "The Securities Act and Its Effect upon the Institutional Investor," *Law and Contemporary Problems*, IV: 80 (1937).

Landis, James M., *The Administrative Process*, New Haven, 1938.

Lasser, J. K., and Gerardi, J. A., *Federal Securities Act*, New York, 1934.

Laws: The Securities Act of 1933; The Securities Exchange Act of 1934; The Trust Indenture Act of 1939; The National Bankruptcy Act.

Lee, Richard, "The Financial House and Its Customers," *Boston University Law Review*, 15: 234 (1935).

Lincoln, Edmond, *Applied Business Finance*, Revised Edition, New York, 1941.

Lyon. Hastings, *Corporations and Their Financing*, New York, 1938.

May, George, "The Position of Accountants under the Securities Act," *Journal of Accountancy*, 57: 9 (1934).

MacChesney, Brunson, "The Securities Act and the Promoter," *California Law Review*, 25: 66 (1936).

MacChesney, Brunson, and O'Brien, Robert, "Full Disclosure under the Securities Act," *Law and Contemporary Problems*, IV: 133 (1937).

Mead, E. S., Jeremiah D. B., and Warrington, W. E., *The Business Corporation*, New York, 1941.

Moulton, H. G., *Financial Organization and the Economic System*, New York, 1938.

Neff, Harold H., "Forms for Registration of Securities under the Acts of 1933 and 1934," *Harvard Law Review*, 51: 1354 (1938).

Nielson, Siegvald, "The Issuance of Securities under the English Companies Act," *Virginia Law Review*, 20: 88 (1933).

Palmer, Sir Francis, *Company Law*, 15th Edition, London, 1933.

Publications of the Securities and Exchange Commission: a. Annual Reports, 1935, 1936, 1937, 1938, 1939, 1940; b. Decisions, Vols. 1 to 7 inclusive; c. Official Summaries of Security Transactions and Holdings of Officers, Directors, and Principal Stockholders; d. Releases under (1) Securities Act, (2) Securities Exchange Act, (3) Bankruptcy Act, (4) Trust Indenture Act; e. Rules, Regulations and Forms (1) General Rules and Regulations under the Securities Act, (2) Guide to the Forms Adopted under the Securities Act, (3) Handbook to the Registration Record, (4) Rules of Practice; f. Special Studies (1) *Report on the Study of Investment Trusts and Investment Companies*, (2) *Report on the Study and Investigation of the Work, Activities, Personnel and Functions of Protective and Reorganization Committees*, (3) *Cost of Flotation of Small Issues, 1925-1929 and 1935-1939*, (4) *Cost of Flotation for Registered Securities, 1938-1939.*

Ripley, W. Z., *Main Street and Wall Street*, Boston, 1927.

Rodgers, Churchill, "Purchase by Life Insurance Companies of Securities Privately Offered," *Harvard Law Review*, 52: 773 (1939).

Samuel, Horace, *Shareholders' Money*, London, 1933.

Sanders, T. H., "Accounting Aspects of the Securities Act," *Law and Contemporary Problems*, IV: 191 (1937).

Security Markets, New York, 1935.

Seligman, Eustace, "Amend the Securities Act," *Atlantic Monthly*, 153: 370 (1934).

Smith, Russell, "The Relation of Federal and State Securities Laws," *Law and Contemporary Problems*, IV: 241 (1937).

Starkey, Rodney, "Practice under the Securities Act of 1933 and the Securities Exchange Act of 1934 from the Viewpoint of the Accountant," *Journal of Accountancy*, 58: 431 (1934).

Stone, Justice Harlan, "The Public Influence of the Bar," *Harvard Law Review*, 48: 1.

Testimony of Expert Witnesses at S. E. C. Hearings, *Journal of Accountancy*, 67: 199, 279 (1939)

Throop, Allen, and Lane, Chester, "Some Problems of Exemption under the Securities Act of 1933," *Law and Contemporary Problems,* IV: 89 (1937).

Uniform Accounting Requirements for Financial Statements, Chicago, 1940.

U. S. Department of Commerce, *Trade Promotion Series No. 153* (1935).

Watson, Deneen, "The Federal Securities Act from the Viewpoint of the State Securities Commissioner," *Certified Public Accountant,* 13: 599 (1933).

Willis, H. P., and Bogen, J. I., *Investment Banking,* Revised Edition, New York, 1936.

INDEX